Shetland Sheepdogs
An Owner's Companion

SHETLAND SHEEPDOGS
AN OWNER'S COMPANION

Malcolm Hart

The Crowood Press

First published in 1999 by
The Crowood Press Ltd
Ramsbury, Marlborough
Wiltshire SN8 2HR

British Library Cataloguing-in-Publication Data
A catalogue record for this book is available from the British Library.

ISBN 1 86126 199 3

Throughout this book, 'he', 'him' and 'his' have been used as neutral pronouns and refer to both males and females.

Line-drawings by author, except those on pages 51 and 53, which are by Elizabeth Mallard-Shaw.

Edited and designed by OutHouse Publishing Services.

Printed and bound in Great Britain by Redwood Books.

Contents

Acknowledgements

So many people have given freely of their time and support during the many years of research for this book that it is impossible to name them all. They know who they are and they have my sincere thanks.

Special acknowledgement is due to the Sheltie devotees in other countries who have so willingly provided information and material without which I could not have traced the progress of the Shetland Sheepdog in his adopted lands – Aud Jorun and Helge Lie in Norway, Fleming Larsson in Denmark, Madeleine Lund, Birgita Svarstaad and Carin Akkasan in Sweden, Guy Jeavons in South Africa, and Barbara and Jeff Phillips in Australia. The encyclopaedic knowledge of Mary Davies has helped to fill many gaps in my knowledge.

Thanks are also due to those who have entrusted me with precious photographs and given permission to publish them, and to the English Shetland Sheepdog Club for their permission to reproduce the extended Breed Standard.

Finally, to my wife Patti and son Neil, for their unstinting support, encouragement and sometimes necessary bullying, as well as their patience in moments of self-doubt, my deepest gratitude.

1

History of the Breed

Many new owners of Shetland Sheepdogs have a rather romantic notion of their puppies' ancestors. They envisage golden, glamorous, eager-to-please little dogs, sitting at the feet of plaid-wrapped shepherds on a windswept northerly island. My wife Patti and I certainly had this sort of picture in our minds, but the romance lasted only as long as it took us to read our first book on the breed. It told us that the late Miss Day Curie, an early supporter of the breed, described Shetland Sheepdogs she had seen at a show in Glasgow in 1908, as little mongrels about eight to ten inches in height.

Many accounts of how the breed evolved have been written, but the lack of hard evidence has given birth to all sorts of theories and suppositions, none of them easy to substantiate or refute. The truth remains as elusive as it was at the beginning of the twentieth century. The first book about the breed, written in 1916 by Miss Beryle Thynne of the Kilravock Shetland Sheepdogs, says 'the original specimens of the breed were really mongrels that were used for the purpose of herding cattle, ponies and sheep indigenous to the Islands.' It includes letters sent to her by breeders on the Shetland Islands and the mainland who claimed to have studied the breed, but the information contained in the letters is largely conjectural and often contradictory.

Old engravings and paintings of Shetland often show dogs as incidental subject matter, not as the main feature. Frustratingly, the dogs range in type from long, low, spaniel-eared dogs to larger, heavier animals who would not look out of place in a modern farmyard. These dogs might be the product of artistic licence, but they might be accurate portrayals.

Early History

All dogs are descended from the wolf. The geneticist Robert Wayne and his team at the University of California have proved this through

DNA testing. Prior to that, some theorists claimed that foxes and jackals had interbred with wolves to produce the canine species.

The transformation from wolf to dog is alleged to have taken place 100,000 years ago. Whatever the time scale, the fact that man and dog evolved together is irrefutable. Cave paintings of hunting scenes clearly show early man and dogs pursuing deer together, and skeletons of dogs have been found intact, not dismembered like those of other small mammals, in close proximity to early settlements.

One of the earliest recognizable types of dog is the Spitz, found mostly in the Northern Hemisphere, where it followed early nomadic tribes. It is reasonable to suppose that dogs evolved different characteristics in different places, depending on the climate and terrain. Archaeological excavations of later settlements have often uncovered carvings and bones of dogs. Finds from Norse settlements are of particular interest to those in search of the Sheltie's origins. The Norse people were originally from Scandinavia, and are best known as Vikings. They were great colonizers, and remains of dogs have been found at Norse sites as far apart as northern Norway and the coastal regions of Normandy in France. These finds are of dogs similar in type to the Elkhound or Buhund, and of another longer-backed, shorter-legged dog which some believe to be the ancestor of the Valhund and Corgi. If the old engravings and paintings of Shetland mentioned above are right, the low, long-cast dog could have played a major role in the formation of the Sheltie. What is certain from the remains is that dogs and other animals were transported as a matter of course from Norse homelands to all Norse colonies.

By 840AD Iceland had been colonized by Norse people, who soon colonized Greenland as well. Around 900 the islands of Shetland and other islands off the coast of Scotland were also settled by Norse people, who introduced their customs and their animals, including dogs. We know that the dogs were of the two types mentioned above. There are few written records of the Norse rule of Shetland – which continued until 1469 when sovereignty of the islands was passed to Scotland – but much more is known about life and dogs on Iceland, which was also under Norse rule and had the same laws, customs and lifestyles.

The main tasks of the Icelandic dogs at that time were to herd ponies, cattle and sheep, and to drive and supervise the trains of pack ponies that carried everything from building stones to harvested crops. The dogs often worked unaccompanied by humans, and their value to Norse settlers was said to be 'that of a good horse'. As the

The Iceland Dog, from the same origins as the original dogs of the Shetland Isles.

numbers of sheep multiplied and the need for hay to sustain animals in winter increased, the dogs were employed to drive sheep in summer to open moorland grazing, away from the hay meadows, and return them to over-winter nearer to the settlements. Any sheep that returned to the hay meadows were chased away most vociferously. It is safe to assume that the dogs of Shetland were employed in much the same way.

In mainland Scotland and England, however, the farmers had more to worry about than marauding sheep. Wolves and bears abounded in the heavily wooded countryside, as did desperate bands of men living 'outside of the law'. So a dog much larger than the herding dogs of Iceland was required to protect sheep, cattle and the inhabitants of the small settlements. The Celts, in their migration across Europe,

The Scottish Sheepdog or shepherds dog introduced to Shetland circa 1760.
Print taken from an authenticated painting dated 1750.

brought with them just such a dog, probably descended from the Persian Sheepdogs. Much later, the Romans brought more of these dogs to swell the ranks. These dual-purpose herding and protection dogs were instrumental in the development of the intensive farming and stock-rearing culture that flourished from the beginning of the twelfth century.

As the wolf population was reduced – the last survivor in England was allegedly despatched in 1560 quite near to our home – these large dogs became surplus to requirement. However, free enterprise found alternative employment for them – at great cost to the King's deer! Such was the problem posed by poachers and their dogs that it was deemed necessary to limit the size of dog that peasants were allowed to own; it was reasoned that the smaller the dog, the lower the chance of its being capable of running down deer. To enforce this restriction, a 'dog gauge' was used to determine whether a dog fell below a maximum height and size. This gauge took the form of a metal hoop through which the dogs of the low born had to pass. Any that were too large to do so were summarily despatched or maimed. (It is thought by some that this practice gave rise to the expression, 'to be put through the hoop'.)

The increase in stock-rearing meant that a different type of dog was required to control and herd the ever-growing number of sheep, and this was found in the mountainous western part of Britain (which was coincidentally the area most successfully settled by the Norse who integrated readily with existing tribes). Believed to be about sixteen inches (40cm) in height – and so able to pass through the metal-hoop measure – this dog was responsive, quick and clever, and became popular with shepherds from further afield. It was eventually to develop into the Border Collie, revered to this day for its amazing prowess with sheep and unsurpassed talents in obedience and agility competition.

In the meantime Shetland was ceded to Scotland in 1469 as part of the marriage treaty between Margaret, Princess of Denmark, and James III of Scotland. The proviso for the transference was that the laws and customs of the islands would remain unaltered. Trade with Scandinavian countries, Greenland and Iceland flourished, and little contact with other countries was necessary. All this was to change in the late 16th century, when control of Shetland passed to the Bishop of Holyrood, in Scotland. He immediately repealed all the laws currently in operation and substituted Scottish rule and custom. Trading with Scandinavia and its colonies ground to a halt, and isolation brought about unforeseen problems for the islands. The already small gene pool of animals, including dogs, was condensed further by lack of contact. The effect of this, combined with the inclement weather and harsh terrain, was to reduce their quality and size so much that visitors to the island commented on the phenomenon. Records of that period state that a single fleece from a Shetland sheep weighed 4½lb (2kg), whereas fleece from mainland Scottish Blackface and Cheviot sheep weighed 6lb (2.7kg). However, this does not take account of the fineness of the Shetland wool: it was so fine that shawls made from it could be drawn through the wedding rings of the women who made them. So Shetland sheep were unlikely to have been much smaller than mainland ones. And claims that the original Shelties were extremely small, and were not required to be larger because the Shetland sheep were 'little bigger than a hare', are clearly wide of the mark. However, action to enlarge the gene pool seemed imperative, and in 1760 the first recorded importation of sheep from the mainland occurred.

The Shetland Sheepdog. Photograph believed to date from 1900–1905.

The Collie Ingredient

It is quite possible that the quick, clever collie so beloved of the mainland shepherds was introduced to Shetland along with the mainland sheep, with the benefit of enlarging the gene pool of the existing island dogs. This first importation of sheep was not wholly successful, though, for the sheep brought with them diseases against which island sheep had no immunity. The new canine recruits, however, are not reported to have had any such calamitous effects. The infusion of collie genes appears only to have modified the appearance of the original, spitz-like, island dogs, so that they looked more like collies.

In 1820 the Highland Clearances reached Shetland, having already changed vast areas of Scotland from small family-run farms, or crofts, into huge sheep-farming units. The new large-scale sheep farming meant that sheep were introduced in greater numbers from the mainland, and with them came shepherds and dogs with experience in handling larger flocks. This influx of shepherd dogs must have further modified the appearance of the original Norse types of Shetland.

The resulting dogs have been described to me by descendants of crofters, including one man who actually worked on his family croft before his under-age enlistment in the Royal Navy. 'Not much bigger than they are today,' is one description, and given the difficulty many people seem to have in estimating height I am inclined to think the dogs may have been even larger. 'Quarrelsome and not kindly disposed,' is another comment, which is surprising given the delightful nature of Shelties today. The dogs are described as 'much shorter in the muzzle, and mostly black and white, although some crofters preferred black and tan. The tan markings were often similar to those seen on German Shepherds.' The descriptions also highlight the difference in coat: the working dogs had short, harsh coats, and any longer-coated dogs would have to suffer the indignity of having their coats cut short or smeared with pig fat so that they would not become waterlogged or collect balls of mud or snow. It is interesting to note that shepherds who farm today in the Lake District in the north of England (where I live) still prefer 'slape', as the smooth-coated dogs are called in the local dialect. It is not unknown for a heavier-coated dog to be smeared with axle grease to repel mud and snow.

Introduction to the Mainland

With these descriptions and photographs from the end of the nineteenth century, it is difficult to imagine how a cottage industry sprang up, supplying tiny, fluffy dogs to visitors to the islands, and yet it did. My contacts were scathing about such practices, saying that the puppies carried back to England and Scotland as native dogs were 'No such thing and reflected no credit on the producers nor the visitors who bought them without finding out if they were at all typical.' Scepticism about the authenticity of these early imports was voiced publicly too. In early 1909 the publication *Collie Folio* printed a number of scathing articles and letters about the new and emerging Shetland Collie, claiming in one article, 'Our informant learns from a regular visitor to The Shetlands that the dealers in dogs there obtain cast-off Pomeranians from Aberdeen to sell as Shetland Collies, which in all probability will be used to breed from and perpetuate this absurdity.' Individuals were named in these articles, but there is no case of libel on record.

The trade in puppies increased despite opposition from traditionalists. Horse traders, who went to the islands to buy Shetland ponies for mainland coal mines, were commissioned by clients in both Scotland and England to bring back puppies as well. A trader called Mr Clark founded the Ashbank kennel of Shetland Sheepdogs, and became one of the breed's earliest pioneers.

Some owners of these newly imported dogs were anxious to discover the history of the dogs on the islands, and due to the absence of known facts and perhaps some deliberate misinformation, many fanciful theories were accepted as true. The island breeders were credited with mating their bitches with dogs from visiting yachts and ships from Holland and Germany. There were stories about whaling ships bringing in the Greenland Yaki dog, which came from Norse stock possibly crossed with a pre-Norse sled dog. One story that is still widely believed is that a lustful King Charles Spaniel jumped ship in the Shetland Islands and entertained a selection of local bitches. It is little wonder that Miss Thynne wrote in her book that 'the history of the Shetland Sheepdog is wropt in mystery.'

In the years when Shetland dogs were arriving on the mainland, many breeds were already undergoing 'improvement' by dedicated enthusiasts with time and money to spend. What exactly occurred when these improvements were extended to the Sheltie is anybody's guess. Stories abound that a large white Pomeranian was used, and this is easy to believe, given that prick ears and round skulls still appear. Older breeders tell of seeing a Papillon mated to a bitch in one of the pioneering kennels, and there is another account of a blue roan Cocker Spaniel's contribution to the gene pool. The low-set, heavy ears fairly often seen on merle Shelties give substance to this rumour.

The uncertainty that surrounds these early times for the breed becomes a frustrating mystery for the dedicated historian. Sheltie pioneers in the early 20th century were generally wealthy and well-educated women, and such women often kept detailed daily journals. The absence of any such data on the Sheltie is surprising, and it is possible that some written records do still exist, and are waiting to be discovered. For the time being, it is impossible to give a detailed account of the most important part of the development of the Shetland Sheepdog. The only breed known for certain to have been used is the Rough Collie. This had itself been the recipient of fairly intensive improvement, with the introduction of the Borzoi to refine and elongate the head, the Gordon Setter for its distinctive tricolour markings, and possibly the Irish Setter, to 'brighten up the sables'.

A Miss Humphries of the Mountfort kennel is known to have purchased and used a small Collie bitch called Teena before reselling her to Mr Jim Saunders, whose important part in the development of the breed is described below. Few other breeders confessed to similar

Fipinella of Mountfort, by Warbaby of Mountfort out of Suzette of Mountfort, born 31 October 1919.

projects, and we may never know to what extent Collie crosses were used, or for how long. Some breeders believe that at least one kennel was still using Collies into the 1950s and possibly the 1960s, to eradicate the dreaded round skull.

The fluctuations in size and type resulting from infusions of Collie and other blood resulted in furious conflict between the Shetland Collie Club, founded in 1908, the Scottish Shetland Sheepdog Club, founded in 1909, and the English Shetland Sheepdog Club, founded in 1914. Two separate registers were kept, one for dogs measuring 10–12in (25.5–30cm), and the other for dogs measuring 12–15in (30–38cm). Some breeders felt that standardizing type and size was an impossible task, and campaigned for two distinct varieties of the breed to be recognized by the Kennel Club. Show judges intensified the problem. Dogs thought more typical of the original Sheltie would win one week but do badly the next, when new and improved Shelties would take the awards.

15

The Kennel Club had many doubts that these dogs could ever be standardized sufficiently to meet its criteria, but at the end of 1914 it dropped its objections and granted official recognition to the breed. The Rough Collie clubs had taken exception to the name Shetland Collie, the original and most popular choice, so it was as the Shetland Sheepdog that the breed with its past 'wropt in mystery' and many more 'improvements' still to come, became legitimate.

Development of the Modern Breed

In 1909, the Ladies Kennel Association became the first English show to schedule separate classes for the breed, and generated great interest in the Sheltie among a number of breeders. Shelties had already become a fairly regular sight at Scottish shows.

The outbreak of the First World War in 1914 had no apparent effect on showgoing. During that year, a dog called Woodvold, whose dam was a

Capt. and Mrs Hauffmann with their Shepherds Shelties, and their kennel maid Countess Schtesia (centre), Gothenburg 1947.

16

Three early Swedish Shelties. Stormkapperns Diamond, Irene and Beauty.

small Collie named Greta, was regularly shown. So was Wallace, whose unregistered sire 'Butcher Boy' became the founder, through Wallace, of the BB male line. Woodvold, a tricolour with not much in the way of white markings, became a champion in 1916. Wallace failed to win any Challenge Certificates (CCs), but he was to be vitally important to the breed.

In 1915 a black-and-white bitch called Frea won the first CC awarded in the breed, and the tricolour dog Clifford Pat became the breed's first champion in Great Britain. In America, where it seems that dogs of very mixed type and quality had also been imported, Lerwick Rex achieved his American title shortly before Pat. The American Shetland Sheepdog Association has traced the first Sheltie to be registered in the United States as Lord Scott, a sable dog imported directly from Shetland, though I understand neither his parentage nor breeder can be confirmed.

As the war continued and the mood in Britain changed, the Kennel Club decided to suspend shows in 1917, and puppies born in this later part of the war could not be registered. This had a catastrophic effect on what was still very much a breed in its early infancy, and at the end of the war very few Shelties remained.

Miss Humphries, the owner of Wallace, set out to rectify the situation and bought the small golden sable Collie bitch Teena to mate to Wallace. It was accepted that a number of outcrosses to collies had already occurred. Miss Humphries may have wanted to introduce blue merle colouring, as Teena was produced out of a sable bitch by a blue merle dog. Blue merles were allegedly and rather surprisingly unknown on Shetland, despite a solid, silvery-blue colouring being well established in the Scottish Shepherd dogs. If this was Miss Humphries' plan, it failed. Two matings to Wallace failed to produce any blue merles, and Teena passed into the ownership of Jim Saunders.

The first blue merle to appear in the ring was Mrs Baker's bitch Blue Ray of Houghton Hill, who was shown at Crufts in 1926. Her sire was the tricolour Chestnut Rainbow and her dam Blue Floss of Houghton Hill, who we can safely assume was also a blue. Blue Floss's sire and dam are given, intriguingly, as Rover and Gypsy, and her breeder as a Mr Dawson. What breed of dog they were remains a mystery, and Blue Ray appears very different from her contemporaries in her photograph.

Warbaby and Specs

Teena's two matings produced only one survivor, but what an important survivor. Warbaby of Mountfort, as this singleton was registered, was mated to a Wallace daughter, producing the CC-winning Rufus of Mountfort. He was mated to Ko Ko, owned by a Mr McGregor but bred by Jim Saunders out of Teena, whom he mated to another Wallace son, Rip of Mountfort. That litter was the first to have a double injection of Collie blood, or at least the first to have an official and acknowledged double injection, and a small sable dog from it was sold to Miss Humphries. She first intended to call him Great Expectations of Mountfort, but named him Specs of Mountfort instead. I sometimes wonder if Miss Humphries ever regretted her change of mind, as Specs, although it has a friendly, comfortable feel, does little justice to the great effect this dog had, both in the show ring and more importantly as a stud-dog, through his son Ch. Eltham Park Eureka.

Eureka

Originally registered Peter Pan of Mountfort, Eureka passed into the ownership of Mr F. C. Pierce, a successful Collie breeder who had already achieved some success in Shelties, and who promptly changed his name. The dam of Eureka, Princess of Mountfort, was the only sur-

Ch. Haytimer of Hanburyhill at Harlmere, bred by Mrs R. Archer, and owned by Rev. and Mrs Hambrey and Patti and Malcolm Hart. (Photo. Mitchell.)

vivor of the two matings between Warbaby of Mountfort and the collie Teena. The three lines Eureka carried to Teena are very obvious in his photographs, and Miss Humphries must have felt elated by this outcome of her breeding plans. One of Eureka's sons, Ch. Max of Clerwood, had a great grandson, Ch. Kinnersley Gold Dust, who in turn sired Fydell Startler.

Fydell Startler

A tricolour with little white, Startler had a most successful puppy career, but was arguably robbed of his title by the Second World War. He won a CC as a veteran in 1947, and there have been twelve male champions to date in direct descent from him, starting with his son Ch. Helensdale Bhan. The others are Champions Helensdale Ace, Hazelhead Gay Wanderer, Penvose Brandy Snap, Riverhill Ratafia, Rodhill Burnt Sugar, Riverhill Ricotta, Haytimer of Hanburyhill at Hartmere, Shelridge Haywire, Lirren Hash Brown, Mohnesee The Sorcerer, and Mohnesee The Illusionist. Another son of Haywire, Ch. Morestyle Moon River, has produced a champion son Morestyle Monsoon, so this successful line continues strongly.

Influential Kennels and Dogs

This survey can give only the outline and highlights. Other books give a comprehensive account of direct descent from both of the major male lines, together with full information on the importance of the twenty-five separate female lines in the early development of the Sheltie. There is a list of recommended reading at the end of this book.

Jim Saunders and the Helensdale Kennel

The immense part played by Jim Saunders and his unswervingly supportive wife Jess in the development of the breed through the Helensdales has not been well recognized. Margaret and Les Dobson of the Doshell Shetland Sheepdogs were close friends of the Saunders and spent a day with us at Hartmere, filled with talk about the Helensdales, shortly before Les died. I have spend fascinating hours immersed in Helensdale memorabilia lent by Margaret, and am indebted to them both. Margaret Dobson handled and showed the last purely Helensdale dog in Britain. Doshell Naiad, rather uncharacteristically a shaded sable, was bred by Margaret and Les and carried their prefix, but was a daughter of Helensdale Golden Gleam by Ch. Sumburgh Sirius. Sirius (out of Ch. Helensdale Vanessa, by Helensdale Frolic, a half-brother to Ch. Helensdale Ace) was bred by Rosemary Morewood, another friend and disciple of Jim Saunders. Her glamorous Sumburgh Shelties attracted many admirers in Britain and overseas in the 1960s and 1970s.

Jim Saunders lived in a small cottage near Aberdeen, where, despite having far less space and fewer resources than many of his contemporaries, he successfully founded a universally recognizable type. I use the word 'type' with care, because Jim strongly believed that the Sheltie should be a collie in miniature. He felt that many breeders were producing incorrect dogs, with two-piece heads, often with domed

Jim Saunders (left) with Helensdale Pamela and Mr G. Clark (Ashbank), one of the earliest importers, with Spendthrift of Exford.

skulls and large, round, protruding eyes. Clever and, it must be said, rather intensive line-breeding soon produced the expression that Jim sought, and further line-breeding 'fixed' the type.

The refined head and oblique almond eyes of the Helensdales, accompanied more often than not by heavy coats of clear gold and sparkling white, found many admirers in the show ring, and success followed success. Always glad to help like-minded enthusiasts, Jim sold many dogs to breeders in Britain and overseas. Dogs went to the Shepherd kennels in Germany, and purchases from this kennel were to have an effect on Scandinavian Shelties. Dogs also went to America, and in particular to Mr William W. Gallagher, who was clearly besotted with Jim's dogs. Such was Jim's reputation as a dog breeder in America that the *New York Post* lead and banner headline on 9 June 1939 was 'Jas. G. Saunders, Aberdeen Scotland welcomed to New York World's Fair'. Further down the page in considerably smaller type were the headlines 'King George at tomb of Washington' and 'King and Roosevelt chat alone'.

Helensdale Frolic.

(Below) *Doshell Naiad, owned by Margaret and Les Dobson.*

Ch. Helensdale Ace.

Ch. Helensdale Ace

Jim's best-known dog was Ch. Helensdale Ace, whose original name, Lone Star, was unaccountably refused by the Kennel Club. Ace came into being because his sire Bhan leaped a fence to mate his own dam, Helensdale Gentle Lady, whose sire Ch. Nicky of Aberlour was the seventh generation from Eureka. This accidental genetic cocktail gave the breed its first Best in Show winner (all breeds) and the first truly influential post-war stud-dog. He sired ten champions and ten others who won CCs but not their titles. His influence might have been much greater, had he not been poisoned by licking weedkiller from his paws after one of his regular forays into a neighbour's garden.

Ace must have been one of the least photogenic dogs ever born. I am assured by all who knew him that although he was certainly not fault-less, his personality and charisma, together with his striking gold colour and glamour, gave him a magic all of his own. No photograph of him catches this. He was a dominant force at stud, and all of his puppies were unmistakably his. Even his crooked white blaze was strongly inherited.

Ace sired six bitches who gained their titles. Perhaps the most important was Riverhill Royal Flush, purchased as a foundation bitch by the sisters Joan and Beryl Herbert, whose prolific Shelert kennel was prominent for almost forty years. Another champion daughter, Shady Fern of Sheldawyn, had a champion grandson, Anchor of Sheldawyn, and both Helensdale Wendy and Waxwing were exported. Miss Todd and the Sheldawyn Shelties are still seen in the show ring to some extent.

Ch. Riverhill Rare Gold

The most prolific of Ace's sons, Ch. Alasdair of Tintobank, who sired eleven champions, was officially bred by Mr W. F. Guthrie, although he actually bought Alasdair's dam, Helensdale Mhairi Dhu, in whelp from Jim Saunders. Alasdair's first champion daughter, Riverhill Rare Gold, a precocious puppy, won her title in three consecutive shows

Ch. and Aust. Ch. Riverhill Rampion. (Photo. Diane Pearce.)

Riverhill Rolling Home. (Photo. C. M. Cooke.)

and became the most important brood bitch in the history of the breed to date. It is impossible to overestimate the effect this amazing bitch has had on the breed. The charts published by the English Shetland Sheepdog Club show only the tail male and female lines, and they do not do full justice to the role she played, although her involvement still appears impressive. Many successful kennels, our own included, owe a tremendous debt to 'Lucy' and her breeders Felicity and Patience Rogers. Her son Ch. Riverhill Rampion was exported to Australia.

The record of thirty champions and a further sixteen CC winners produced by the Rogers sisters between 1934 and 1980, from a not very intense breeding programme, is a virtually unassailable target for aspiring breeders. The figures are impressive, but their contribution to Shelties is colossal, given the influence of Riverhill blood lines in the pedigrees of practically all the winning dogs of today. The Rogers sisters were private and unassuming, although they could be witheringly dismissive of foolish and ill-informed comment at the ringside.

A whole book could be written about 'Lucy' and her descendants. These are only the bare bones of the story. She produced four champion

Ch. Riverhill Royal Flush, the foundation bitch for Shelert Shelties.

daughters to four different stud-dogs, four more daughters who them-selves bred champions, and the CC-winning son Riverhill Rolling Home, who should have won his title and probably would have, but for a desperately unfortunate accident. Rolling Home, or 'Roly', had a most wonderfully outgoing personality, and passed it on in abundance to his children. At that time Shelties were not thought among the bravest of breeds, and I do not think it purely coincidental that temperaments improved dramatically as his influence in breeding plans grew.

Strikin' Midnight at Shelert

'Roly' was the inspired choice of mate for the Herbert sisters' Ch. Slipper Satin of Shelert, herself a cleverly bred bitch with several lines back to Ace and Ch. Riverhill Redcoat, another most influential sire. A 14in (35.5cm) tricolour male was retained, and given the name Strikin' Midnight at Shelert. He was shown with some success and achieved a Reserve CC, but it was as a stud that he really excelled, siring eleven champions. To this day, he is the only dog to have thrown champions

Shelert champions. **From left:** *Shureen, Streak Lightening, Such a Spree, Such a Beano, Special Edition, with their sire, Strikin' Midnight at Shelert. (Photo. Bertram Unne.)*

in the three principal colours. He had particularly neat ears that he passed on to all of his progeny, most importantly the merles, who at that time had conspicuously untidy ears. The extra look of quality in his merle offspring soon brought rich rewards in the show ring, for both his home kennel and others fascinated by this difficult and demanding colour. His merle sons Ch. Such a Spree at Shelert and Ch. Scylla Vaguely Blue (Marion Marriage's cleverly and bravely named dog) have contributed to the success of the Felthorn kennel of Barbara and Dick Thornley, the Rockarounds of Jean Angel, and Sandy Tinker's Ruscombe kennel. The influence of these kennels has played a large part in elevating the merles to their strong position in the show ring.

The Freelancer Head

Another son of 'Roly' was Ch. Antoc Sealodge Spotlight. His son Glenmist Golden Falcon mated Ch. Heathlow Luciana, bred by the late Heather Lowe but owned by Cath and Allan Jeffries, who had already been extremely successful with their Rough Collies. Luciana was virtually all Helensdale and Aberlour bred. A resultant puppy, Jefsfire Freelancer, a bright golden sable with a captivating head and expression,

The first three generations of champion bitches. From left: *Ch. Riverhill Rare Gold, Ch. Riverhill Rarity of Glenmist, Ch. Gypsy Star of Glenmist.*

made a tremendous impact in the show ring and gained his title with ease. He was much sought after as a stud, and his offspring invariably inherited his good head, soon referred to as a 'Freelancer Head'.

Janetstown Kennel

The Janetstown Shelties owned by Jan Moody, based on a combination of Helensdale and Riverhill lines, have produced a steady stream of sable champions, all with a distinctive and easily recognizable Janetstown stamp. The top-winning bitch of her time, Ch. Jasmine of Janetstown, a double granddaughter of Ch. Mistmere Marching Orders, has also proved her worth as a brood through her son Janetstown Jorrocks, sired by Ch. Scylla Scottish Rifle. Jorrocks sired Ch. Jazzman of Janetstown, who is behind a number of champions in his own and other kennels.

Whitelaw Kennel

The Whitelaw kennel of Margaret Heatley was also based firmly on Helensdale lines. Her Ch. Laird of Whytelaw was a son of Ace and is in the pedigrees of many top dogs of today. The lasting qualities of the breed were demonstrated when Ch. Skye of Whytelaw won his last CC under Mona McConnel of Shelverne fame, at almost ten years of age. He looked magnificent.

The CHE Line

The dogs named above are all from the BB (or Butcher Boy) line, but although this was enormously influential it cannot claim sole respon-sibility for the breed. Many kennels owe their success to the CHE line descending from the little tricolour Ch. Uam Var of Houghton Hill, principally through his grandson Ch. Riverhill Rufus, and Rufus's grandson Ch. Viking of Melvaig, father of Ch. Dilhorne Norseman of Melvaig and Ch. Wattawoodcut.

These include Mrs Charlesworth's Dilhorne kennel of tricolours and merles, and the Exfords of Colonel and Mrs Sangster, whose belief in sound construction and rigorous exercise brought alive the Breed Stan-dard phrase 'covering the maximum ground with the minimum of effort'. The Greenscrees kennel of Bill and the late Rita Henry, who spe-cialized in sables, was also a potent force, and was instrumental in the success of many of the modern kennels described below.

Britain

Callart and Milesend

Miss Olwen Gwynne Jones's Callart kennel was influential in the devel-opment of the breed, and despite a period away from the show ring the Callarts still win awards, notable the sable dog Callart the Dancing Flames, a son of the prolific Milesend Trivial Pursuit, owned by Mrs Joyce Miles. Joyce is a convert from her original love, the Rough Collie, and came to Shelties when she bought Myriehewe Magic Moments of Miles-end from the Beaden sisters. He was a son of Monkswood Maestro of Lyngold out of Rodhill Elfin Moon, so Joyce's appreciation of the River-hill type was immediately fixed. Progressive line-breeding through the propitiously bought Monkswood Magic Flute of Milesend has produced enviable success with a series of dogs and bitches who are remarkably alike – the result of line-breeding for quality heads and correct construc-tion. Her Ch. Milesend Storm Warden, who attained his British title at a very young age, was judged Best of Breed at Crufts in 1998, and at the time of writing has been awarded ten CCs. Modestly, Joyce attributes much of her success to Mary Davies, not only for producing Magic Flute but for invaluable advice given freely over the years.

Mary Davies founded the Monkswood kennel in Switzerland but moved it to England. No doubt encouraged and motivated by the presence of her beloved 'Roly', she has produced a succession of champions that unmistakably display the influence of the Riverhills. When a weekly dog publication asked leading breeders to nominate the 'Best Sheltie', several named the lovely tricolour bitch Ch. Greensands Gangsters Moll at Monkswood 'Holly' as either first or second choice. Her sire was Monkswood Marauder, the cleverly named but only lightly shown litter-brother of Ch. Monkswood Moss Trooper, who tragically for the breed had a short stud career. He sired three champions, who inherited their sire's glamour, shape and exquisite expression. Ch. Parrocks Red Dragoon did not breed on, but Ch. Francehill Pin Up produced, to Ch. Jefsfire Freelancer, the sable Ch. Francehill Persimmon, himself an influential sire. The third champion, Mistmere Marching Orders, bred by Sandy Harries, proved to be both a successful show dog and an important sire, whose influence in the pedigrees of many winning kennels cannot be overestimated. His most notable son was Derek and Phyllis Rigby's Ch. Lythwood Snaffles, whose early death, from trying to swallow and bark at the same time confounded the best-laid plans of Hartmere and other kennels. His stud career was far too short for the good of the breed, but Snaffles features strongly in the pedigrees of many of today's winners, and he had the distinction of siring a dog and bitch champion in the same litter.

His kennel mate Ch. Lythwood Skymaster also achieved this rare feat, and shares with Ch. Jefsfire Freelancer the breed record of siring twelve champions. Skymaster's sire was Ch. Sandpiper of Sharval, bred and handled by Albert Wight (see Scotland below), who was achieving fame as a judge of other breeds. Skymaster was the first Sheltie to achieve Best in Show at an all-breeds championship show, and, like Freelancer, was an important stud. His son Ch. Tegwell Wild Ways at Sandwick, bred by Mrs Stanley but owned and campaigned by Chris Mayhewe, sired an impressive list of champions and top-winning dogs and bitches. His progeny have done so well in the ring that he easily won the award of Top Stud Dog All Breeds for 1997. This has never before been achieved by a Sheltie, and the feat is all the more notable given that Shelties produce smaller litters than do many other breeds.

Lythwood is only kennel to date to have bred and owned five generations of champion males; Lythwood Brandysnap, Lythwood Saga,

Lythwood Spruce, Lythwood Scrabble, and Lythwood Steptoe. Scrabble distinguished himself by winning Reserve in the Working Group while still a puppy. At the time of writing, fifteen British Champions have come from this kennel, and a number of CC winners who went on to win titles in other countries.

The Francehills, owned by Margaret Norman (née Searle), have produced an impressive list of twenty-five champions in all three main colours, and quite a number of overseas champions. The dashing boy Ch. Francehill Goodwill had a glittering show career and became one of the then-rare Sheltie winners of the Working Group. Founded on a combination of Exford, Riverhill, and Helensdale lines, the Francehill kennel has produced a stream of winners of easily recognizable, consistent type.

Felthorn is one of many kennels that have benefited from Francehill influences. Felthorn Francehill Pretty Polly, a tricolour bitch by Ch. Dilhorne Blackcap out of the lovely merle Ch. Francehill Glamorous, was purchased in 1963 by Barbara and Dick Thornley, and mated to Francehill Rolling Stone. A tricolour bitch from the mating was mated to Troubleshooter of Shemaur, a product of mainly Shelert breeding, and produced the sable Ch. Felthorn Beachcomber, the winner of seven CCs. Surprisingly this dog played a major part in the founding of the tremendously strong Felthorn blue merle line. Barbara and Dick mated the blue merle Felthorn Puff n' Stuff to him, having failed to conceive from five different tricolour dogs. The litter contained two tricolours, two sable merles, and a tricolour bitch rather unkindly named Felthorn Slack Alice. She was mated to the merle Heathwin Loveable Stewart, a great grandson of Pretty Polly, and out off that union came the tremendous brood bitch Felthorn Marionette.

A small, sound blue merle, Marionette had four litters from matings with the tricolour Shelbrook Moonlighting. Perhaps significantly, only one puppy was born when she was mated to Ruscombe Pipe Down! Her first litter to Moonlighting produced the champion bitches Felthorn Lady, and Felthorn Lady Luck at Morestyle, who is behind Elaine Wilson's two Morestyle sable champions. The second mating produced the Reserve CC-winning Felthorn Ferryman and Felthorn Star Appeal, who became the dam of Ch. Ruebecia Orion, influential in the Ruscombe Shelties. The third litter included the blue Ch. Button Moon and the tricolour Harvest Moon, who became an Australian Champion, and had a number of Australian Champion offspring. The final mating produced the shapely tricolour bitch Felthorn Moonbeam, the winner of seven Reserve CCs. In addition to

31

other achievements, the kennel has produced four generations of blue merle champion bitches.

The Edglonian kennel of Roy Pearson and his daughter Debbie, the youngest person appointed to award CCs in Britain, was founded in the mid-1970s. The elegance of the Riverhill Shelties prompted the purchase of a daughter of Riverhill Ring Money, by the influential Ch. Mistmere Marching Orders. A mating to Ch. Riverhill Ricotta, an underused dog (based in the North of England), produced Edglonian Martini Sweet, who won a Reserve CC, and her brother Edglonian Minstrel Boy of Newsprig, who became the sire of champions.

Rhinog Rather Elegant, a beautifully bred puppy, was purchased at the suggestion of Felicity Rogers from Diana Blount, an astute and knowledgeable breeder whose dogs have contributed fresh blood to the breed in many countries. A mating to Minstrel Boy produced Ch. Our Barney of Edglonian, and the champion bitches Edglonian Rather Prity and Edglonian Rather Alluring. Ch. Edglonian Rockin' Robin is a more recent male champion from this kennel of stylish, elegant, line-bred Shelties.

The Mohnesee Shelties were founded by Doreen and Ray Greenhill, with their daughter Kay. The Greenhills first became entranced by Shelties in the very early 1960s, but it was not until 1978 that they could realize their long-cherished wish to breed a litter. Ch. Lythwood Snaffles was their first choice as a stud, and a bitch, Mohnesee in the Mood, was retained from the litter. Unusually, seven of the eight champions that this kennel has produced are descended from her. Line-breeding on Ch. Jefsfire Freelancer lines through his son Ch. Francehill Persimmon brought immediate success, and further line-breeding through Snaffles, via his grandson Ch. Lythwood Skymaster, brought further honours. A slight change in direction was brought about through Ch. Lirren Hashbrown, and resulted in Ch. Mohnesee the Sorcerer, who in turn sired Ch. Mohnesee the Illusionist.

Herds is an historic affix owned now by Mary Gatheral. It was originally in the possession of her father, who did not breed Shelties. Mary owns one of the joint holders of the current breed record for challenge certificates – thirty four at the time of writing. Ch. Herds. the Helmsman is a heavily coated sable and white, but two previous Herds champions, Herriot and Hurdler, were tricolour. Herds breeding is based on a sound working knowledge of Riverhill lines, with the judicious influx of new blood. The kennel currently has two very promising bitches.

Ch. Herds Heatherbelle at Beckwith was purchased as a puppy by Kath and Dave Macmillan, who also admire the Riverhill lines. They bred from her the lovely Ch. Beckwith Bit of a Glama Girl. Line-breeding has produced several other Beckwith champions and CC winners, including the tricolour former breed CC record holder, Ch. Cultured at Cashella, owned and handled by Angela Johnstone.

Ch. Beckwith Bit of a Vagabond at Shelmyth, another handsome tricolour and a lovely mover, was acquired and handled to his title by Rosanne Smith. She founded the Shelmyths on the bitch Beckwith Be Little Be Good who produced, to Ch. Hartmere Harris Tweed, the sable bitch Ch. Shelmyth Sweet Expression. She in turn produced a son, Ch. Shelmyth Special Blend, to Ch. Monkreddon Royal Blend. This small kennel has a tremendous success rate. Joywil Jingle won a CC, and Shelmyth Special Edition, by Ch. Haytimer of Hanburyhill at Hartmere, who was desperately unfortunate not to gain his title, but won two CCs and four Reserve CCs.

Another of Yorkshire's quality Sheltie kennels is Pat and Martin Griggs's Ceirrhig Shelties. Pat and Martin combined their original Kyleburn lines with the predominantly Riverhill blood of Beckwith to produce the heavily coated tricolour dog Ch. Ceirrhig Cragsman. Ch. Ceirrhig Calypso, so elegant and feminine, came soon after, as did the bitch champions Confusion (by Cragsman), and Controversy (by a son of Cragsman out of Calypso). Other CC and Reserve CC-winning bitches continue this productive line.

Denise Rowan's Rowancrest Shetland Sheepdogs produced the lovely Ch. Gold Illusion at Rowancrest, out of an Edglonian bitch by Kelmstone Shades of Gold, who carried Willow Tarn and Westaglow blood lines. Mated to Ch. Tegwell Wild Ways of Sandwick, Gold Illusion gave Denise the charming sable dog Ch. Rowancrest Regality. Gold Illusion was then mated with the Widways son Ch. Herds The Helmsman and produced another sable dog, Rowancrest Just Simply Red, who was bought and campaigned to his title by the Munro family, based in Scotland.

June Scott and the Penrave Shelties, near neighbours of Rowancrest, bred the tricolour dog Ch. Penrave Private Benjamin, who was rich in Francehill blood and was owned and campaigned by Denise Rowan to become her first champion. June both bred and campaigned the tricolour bitch Ch. Penrave Penny Black, whose lines are completely Riverhill. A succession of tricolour and merle top winners have followed. Kath Shovelton bred the lovely merle bitch Dunbrae Miss Dior of Penrave by Penrave Private Eye out of Dunbrae Belinda in Blue, and June campaigned her to her title.

Gwen and Irene Beaden have achieved tremendous success with their Myriehewe Shetland Sheepdogs (and also their Collies). They wisely bought Rodhill Elfin Moon, a tricolour bitch of impeccable Riverhill breeding (she was a granddaughter of Rare Gold) from the late Josie Rae. Of the thirteen champions produced to date from this kennel, no less than seven are descended directly from Elfin Moon, including the amazing Ch. Myriehewe Rosa Bleu. Rosa has won thirty-four CCs, the most ever won by a bitch, and shares the breed record with The Helmsman. She has achieved unparalleled success at Group level in her career, having been placed top in the Working Group seven times, including twice in consecutive years at Crufts. She was twice Best in Show and twice Reserve Best in Show at general championship shows, and twice Sheltie of the Year. Among her many attributes, her sparkling blue colour and gorgeous coat attracted the attention of breed specialists and all-round judges alike, and her outstanding showmanship and ring presence helped take her constantly to the top. All these successes in the show ring are, however, meagre compensation for the fact that Rosa underwent emergency surgery as a very young puppy to avert a life-threatening pyometra, and cannot be bred from. The stud-dogs Ch. Ferdinando of Myriehewe and Ch. Crisanbee Goldsmith of Myriehewe are prominent in the pedigrees of many currently successful dogs.

The long-established Snabswood kennel of Ron and Jean Fitzsimmons has used the very best Greenscrees bloodlines, combined with much Ellington breeding. The elegant Ch. Greencrees Nobleman was the sire of Ch. Snabswood Slainthe, who sired Ch. Snabswood Summer Wine at Willow Tarn. Summer Wine was made up by Ros Crossley, and when mated to Ch. Marksman of Ellendale produced Ch. Solveig of Snabswood. Snabswood Shiny Penny is a promising bitch; Snabswood Sandbagger, a son of Marksman, had a successful puppy career and took a Reserve CC, before leaving for Australia, where he appears in many pedigrees.

Ros Crossley's Willow Tarn Shelties had been shown with considerable success, before the arrival of her Ch. Willow Tarn Telstar, a beautifully bred dog whose lines back through Moss Trooper and Rhinog/Riverhill were apparent. Telstar sired the elegant bitch Ch. Willow Tarn True Love, whose breeding owed much to the Philhope kennel of the talented and much-missed Phyl Pierce. Snabswood Summer Wine gave Ros the lovely Ch. Willow Tarn Tear Maria, sired by Ch. Forestland Target (himself sired by Snabswood Sandbagger before the latter went 'down under'). A great-grandson of True Love, the CC-winning Willow Tarn Trueman (a son of Exbury Yorrick), is important because he is genetically clear of CEA (Collie Eye Anomaly) as well as for his Westaglow lines. He is the sire of the latest Willow Tarn champion – Springcrest Lucky Titus from Willow Tarn.

The Forestland Shelties of Rosemary Marshall came to prominence with the CC-winning Forestland Honeysuckle, a bitch with a considerable amount of Sumburgh (and thus Helensdale) blood. Her mating to Ch. Greenscrees Nobleman produced Ch. Forestland Briar. This super bitch was then mated to Snabswood Sandbagger, and excelled herself by giving Rosemary the elegant litter brother and sister Champions Target and Tassel. The Forestland versatility is exemplified by the more recently crowned merle Ch. Forestland Emperor Moth.

Christine Aaron's Shelridge kennel has been active and successful for more than thirty years. The splendidly headed Ch. Shelridge Haywire, by Haytimer out of Shelridge Soothsayer, adorns the front of this book. Soothsayer, a super brood bitch, also produced the elegant, and very beautiful Ch. Shelridge Ceildh, a particular favourite of mine. Shelridge Socrates, from the same strong line, is the sire of our latest champion, Hartmere Hallmarked, out of the dual CC-winning Hartmere Hidden Gold. Shelridge Gatecrasher, a handsome tricolour, consistently won placings in an era when competition from the largest kennels was at its fiercest. He was sired by the equally handsome tricolour Ch. Hildlane Winters Night, and is behind many top winners of today. Another competitor of those times, the merle Shelridge Liberty Belle had the same sire, and unusually is in the pedigrees of many sable champions. Ch. Shelridge Sunflower is an ultra-feminine bitch with a particularly sweet expression. She was virtually unbeatable during a glittering puppy career, the high spot of which was winning Best Puppy in Show under the world-renowned all-round judge Terry Thorn, at the National Working Breeds.

Lyn French of the Lirren Shelties has bred an enviable number of winning dogs, despite keeping only small numbers. Her first champion was the tricolour Lirren Evening Shadow at Ramptin, owned and campaigned by the Martins. After a break from the show ring, the Lirrens re-emerged with Ch. Hartmere Hayday at Lirren, by Haytimer out of Ch. Hebson Galeforce at Hartmere, litter sister to Ch. Hartmere Heather. Ch. Lirren Hash Brown, a son of Ch. Shelridge Haywire, was used to some effect by the Morestyle and Mohnesee Shelties; and the lovely Ch. Lirren Paper Moon had a CC-winning Lirren Paper Boy.

Another kennel re-emerging after a period away from the show ring is Rannerdale, owned by Anne and Dudley Stafford. The very distinctive type bred here is exemplified by the champion males Rannerdale

Bertie Wooster and Rannerdale Golden Shot. The CC-winning Rannerdale Hot Shot was acquired by the great Sheltie enthusiast Professor Markie, who campaigned him on the Continent.

Scottish Kennels

The long-established Vaila kennel of Margaret and the late Ian Anderson, was founded on Lydwell and Riverhill lines, and has produced an impressive list of winning dogs. Most prominent in my memory is the heavily coated tricolour Vaila Easter Advocaat, a CC winner, and the beautifully coloured merle Vaila Blue Sparkling Hock. Always named after alcoholic beverages, the Vailas were campaigned without regard for distance.

Albert Wight always handled and presented his Sharval Shelties to a high standard, and I suspect this reflected his blossoming interest in breeds for which the value of thorough preparation for the show ring was understood and appreciated rather more than among Sheltie-exhibitors at that time. Ring technique and immaculate presentation alone do not ensure success, however, and the hallmark of this successful exhibitor was sound construction with free-flowing movement, shown by the Sharval champions The Delinquent, Sandpiper (the first Sheltie to win Best in Show at a general championship show), Small Dark and Handsome (exported to Holland after gaining his title), and the bitch Merle Oberon – cleverly named, as were all the Sharval dogs. Another successful Sharval product was the sable bitch Sharval Copper Cream (by Haytimer), who was retired from the ring after winning two CCs.

Another long-established kennel is Nan and Harry Wheeler's Harribrae Shetland Sheepdogs. Until very recently it specialized in sables, and I have often wondered if this could have been a major factor in the sweet expressions for which it has such a reputation. With seemingly apparent ease, the Wheelers produce winning dogs that are so alike it is almost impossible to single out any outstanding individual, but my own favourite was Harribrae Hallmark. He followed an impressive puppy career by winning a CC, but then tragically fell victim to Parvovirus, which had a devastating effect on a number of kennels before a vaccine was developed. The latest star of this kennel is the CC-winning bitch Japaro Sound of Music at Harribrae (a daughter of Ch. Mohnesee the Sorcerer), bred by Margo and Ian Nixon. The Japaro Shelties quickly acquired the winning habit, and the Nixons are the owner-breeders of the sable bitch Japaro Offbeat Jazz, by Ch. Monkreden Royal Blend out of a Harribrae bitch. She took her title after a consistent show career.

In Fife is the long-established Rivvalee kennel, owned by Anne Wyse, whose first major success came at Crufts in 1985, with the pretty sable bitch Orean Careena. Always refreshingly self-effacing, Anne was completely overcome when judge Beryl Herbert (of Shelert fame) handed her the CC, and fainted into the arms of ring steward Robin Searle. Many more winners have come from Rivvalee since that day, in particular the blue merle dog Ir. Ch. Rivvalee Honeymoon Cruise, and the aptly named bitch Rivvalee Blue Mist, who has two CCs to her credit to date.

Orean Carena was bred by the Smith family (also in Fife), who have bred and successfully shown several Shelties, all bearing a striking resemblance to each other. Among the current show team, the shaded sable dog Orean Rainbow Warrior has two CCs to his credit.

Michael Ewing's Sommerville Shetland Sheepdogs kennel is in Ayrshire. The graceful golden sable bitch Sommerville Seed Pearl won the CC at the English Shetland Sheepdog Championship Show while still a puppy. The Reserve CC-winning Japaro D'Joker of Sommerville sired the precocious bitch Sommerville Sunrise, a Reserve CC winner at nine months.

Ellonyorn Shelties have been a mainstay of the breed in Scotland for many years. One of its winning dogs is the lovely tricolour Ch. Kyleburn Penny Black.

Scandinavia

The Shetland Sheepdog is one of the most numerically strong show dogs in many countries, and is in an extremely strong position in all the countries of Scandinavia.

Sweden

In 1930, Captain Einar Hauffmann and his wife Anna started their Shepherds kennel at Skane, in southern Sweden, by importing the tricolour dog Connis of Redbraes, destined to become the first Swedish Champion in 1933. Connis was purchased from Misses Beryl Thynne and Clara Bowring, early pioneers of the breed in Britain, and was soon followed by the two sable bitches Kilravoc Mignonette and Larkbeare Apricot Flan. Captain Hauffmann then imported two blue merles apparently during the Second World War, from the Houghton Hill kennel of Mrs Baker. Two influential sires produced by Captain Hauffmann in the 1940s were Ch. Shepherds Nick-Nack and his son Shepherds Kilham. Jim Saunders and Captain Hauffmann developed a close friendship, which resulted in a number of Helensdales joining the Shepherds kennel. It had an influence on the breed until 1960.

After the Second World War, interest in the breed increased steadily. Birgitta Osttergren's Stormkappen kennel imported Ch. Fydell Round Robin, heavily line-bred to Ch. Nicky of Aberlour, who was joined later by Fydell Harvestmoon, in whelp to Ch. Helensdale Bhan. Each of the resultant litter became Swedish champions, as did Round Robin, who sired excellent stock, including the popular stud-dog Int. Nord. Ch. Stormkappens Diamond.

In Sweden as in other countries, Collie enthusiasts were attracted to the Sheltie. The Pukedals kennel of Ingrid Engstrom imported dogs from Callart bloodlines, and the influential Heathlow Lathmere Elvan (a son of Ch. Penvose Brandy Snap), who gained his title, only to become disappointingly sterile at an early age. Combinations of these imports with the best of the Shepherds bloodlines were used to great effect by several other kennels during the 1950s and 1960s.

Ruth Werner of the Skaraberg kennel imported Riverhill Ransom (a son of Ch. Riverhill Rescuer), Ch. Riverhill Rapparee (by Ch. Swagman from Shiel), and Philhope Rich Souvenir (by Ch. Riverhill Richman). All became champions in their adopted land. Rich Souvenir was a popular stud and produced top-winning dogs and bitches.

The Ting-E-Ling kennel of Greta Lindewall, already well known in a number of different breeds, imported Cheluth Echo, Heathlow Audrey (both sired by Ch. Cheluth Twinkleberry), Mantoga Music Master (a son of Helensdale Braw Lad), Heathlow Lear (a tricolour, like his sire Ch. Mantoga Zircon of Kabul), and Lysebourne Telstar (by Ch. Mistmere Marching Orders). All became champions, and they appear in the pedigrees of the current winning kennels of Smedenas, Moorwood, Westpark, Eastdale and Shellricks.

The Manhems Shelties of Lars Englund, formed in 1949 and still active in the breed, imported Riverhill Rolling Home's son Hildlane Night Reveller in 1971. This tricolour dog gained his Nordic title, produced seven champions, and won many progeny classes – and all this despite living in the remote northern part of Sweden.

Birgitta Svarstaad and her mother started the Bifrost kennel in the early 1960s. When Birgitta married Per Svarstaad she registered the enormously influential Moorwood affix, one of only three Swedish

Sheltie kennels to receive the Hamilton Plaquette for distinguished breeding. The very lovely Moorwood Classic Touch of Windside, a daughter of the two imported Rhinogs Gaelic Envoy and Wild Swan, won her title in England, in the expert hands of her owner, Carin Akesson, who lived there for a time.

Among Bifrost's early acquisitions was Nord. Ch. Mattingley Eve (by Granary Hartfield Handful), and Quendale Crispin (by Ch. Laird of Whytelaw, and produced several champions). The tricolour Nord. Ch. Penvose Black Panther, who despite his colour was heavily line-bred to Ch. Helensdale Ace, sired the tricolour Nord. Ch. Bifrost Sea Master.

In the mid 1970s, Moorwood acquired Rodhill Clouded Moorland (by Riverhill Roux), and Wild Swan of Rhinog (sired by Ch. Rhinog The Gay Lancer). They became international champions and had a great influence on the breeding plans of many kennels. By the end of the decade, they had been joined by Rhinog The Guardian, a tricolour like his sire Ch. Rhinog The Black Watch, and Ingleside Copper Image, both of whom easily gained their International titles. The Guardian sired champions in four colours, and 'Copper', who was twice Sheltie of The Year, was a much used and successful dog who can be found in the pedigrees of many of the winning dogs of today, throughout Scandinavia. Line-breeding to 'Copper' brought more success to the Moorwood kennel, which has also used stock from the talented Australian breeders Barbara and Jeff Phillips, of the Nigma Shelties. When Int. S. N. (Swedish and Norwegian) Ch. Nigma Saffron (by Nigma Nostradamus), was joined by S. Ch. Nigma Honeysuckle (by Aus. Ch. Daestar Dannaher), an immediate impact was made. Int. Nord. Ch. Moorwood Handsome Destiny and Int. S. N. Ch. Moorwood Theme of a Memory are two of several top-winning and top-producing Shelties to result from this venture. Nord. Ch. Nigma Galadrial made the long journey to Carin Akesson, as did Int. NZ & Austral. Ch. Riabel Son of a Gun.

The Smudjenas kennels produced a number of champions towards the end of the 1960s, from mainly Shepherd lines, which were re-inforced by acquisitions from Sumburgh, Snabswood, Forestland and Tegwell.

Ulla Eriksson's Crony kennel began in 1966 with Tumblebays Bewitching (out of Riverhill Rather Smart), who distinguished herself by acquiring her international title and producing several champions to different sires. Other successes include the influential Int. Nord. Ch. Allanvail Gold Express, an imported son of Riverhill Roux, and S. Ch. Milesend Smart Move by Milesend Trivial Pursuit.

Madeleine Lund imported Lythwood Sherry, by Ch. Jefsfire Free-lancer, and Midnightsun Top of The Pops, by Midnightsun Celebra-tion, to found the Starbelle Kennel in 1972. Six years later the kennel acquired Merrymaid Moonlight Madonna, by Int. Nord. Ch. Allan-vail Gold Express, and she headed five generations of champion bitches. Int. S. N. Ch. Starbelle Simply Splendid and Int. S. Dan. Ch. Starbelle Sweet Swan have won reputations both at home and abroad, as has S. Dan. Ch. Stationhill Crackshot, sired by Forestland Target.

Now no longer active, the Westpark Shelties of Gunilla Thiger were founded on Ting-E-Ling lines and achieved great success. Gunilla imported Shelfrect Stroller, by Ch. Midnightsun Justin Time out of Ch. Shelfrect Sunlit Suzanne. He became an International and Nordic Champion and sired an amazing twenty-six champions, and some Obedience Champions. Gunilla also imported another successful show dog, Int. Nord. Ch. Ingleside Golden Cascade, and the British Champion Sulasgar Talamba of Shamaur.

Anna Uthorn founded her Shelgate kennel with the purchase of Int. Nord. Ch. Parrock Pearly Gates (by Ch. Hildlane Winters Night out of Ch. Parrocks Nohow). Mated to her other import Int. Nord. Ch. Delo-raine Dog Star, she produced, among other champions, Int. Nord. Ch. Shelgate Double Diamond, a most consistent winner. His son Nord. Ch. Shelgate Tom Tiddler continued the winning run, and further champions were produced in four colours. Shelgate specialized later in tricolours and merles, several of which were imported from the Rockaround kennel of Jean Angel, notably Ch. Rockaround Sky Blue, who was top brood bitch in 1992/3, producing champions to both Int. S. N. Ch. Shelgate Lucky Devil and the Double Diamond son Int. Nord. Ch. Eastdale Classic Clown.

In 1984 Berit Book and her daughter Jeanette purchased as a puppy the tricolour bitch S. Fin. Ch. Westpark Black Elaine, who was the dam of the above-mentioned Classic Clown. Classic Clown has enjoyed a long and successful show career, and has sired seventeen champions. Eastdale has drawn heavily on foundation stock from the Westpark Shelties to produce champions in all three colours. The purchase of the sable dog S. N. Ch. Mascot, line-bred to Ch. Shelfrect Stroller, has had an impact on this and other kennels.

The Lundecock Shelties of Johnny Anderson, and Ulla Morsing's Gordon Bell kennel, have produced winning Shelties for others as well as themselves during 1990s, and the breed has more strength in depth now than at any other time.

Norway

Norway's dedicated breeders have made giant strides in developing the breed. The first Sheltie to be shown there was Prins, imported from Sweden, who made his appearance in 1948. The first CCs were awarded in 1955, and the bitch winner was Minshells Ballerina, whose parents were bred in Sweden. Sweden was the principal early source for Shelties, but in 1952 Seeboot from Shiel, bred by Margaret Osborne, became the first of many British imports. In 1954, Dagny and Fredrik Matheson, of the Naerstadgaard kennel, imported the sable Riverhill Red Ember (by Ch. Hallinwood Flash out of Riverhill Red Gold). She was in whelp to Ch. Riverhill Rescuer, and in 1956 became the first Norwegian champion.

The Ingeborg Totland's Beautypark kennel and the Bjornstrud's Norsheep kennel imported more Shelties from Britain, and soon established the breed. The Norsk Shetland Sheepdog Klubb gained official recognition in 1964, with Ingeborg as the first president. Despite the dedication and hard work of the first Norwegian Sheltie breeders, only one Norwegian champion and three CC winners had been produced by 1960, but things soon changed dramatically.

The Norsheep kennel imported Barbeque of Exford (a tricolour son of Ch. Lothario of Exford) who won a CC and sired two CC-winning sons before he died tragically young from a brain abscess. Monarch of Monkreddon, by Ch. Laird of Whytelaw, then came to Norsheep after winning a CC in Britain, and gained his Norwegian title. He also sired a Norwegian champion and six CC winners. When Willowstone Water Gypsy joined the kennel, he became both a Norwegian and a Finnish champion, and sired seven CC winners. Willowstone Wiseman (by Riverhill Rolling Home), who already had a CC-winning daughter in England, was then imported. He gained his title and sired a champion and five CC winners. The importance of the early Willowstone imports was confirmed when another Rolling Home daughter, Willowstone Wyndella, was acquired. Although she did not achieve fame in the show ring, she produced two champion daughters whose lines are prominent in both Norway and Finland.

The Beautypark kennel also imported to good effect. Francehill Pickwick, by Ch. Antoc Sealodge Spotlight, produced one champion and six Reserve CC winners. Sharval Boroque, by Ch. Rockaround Blue Gamble, won two CCs. Wildhern Mood Indigo won her Norwegian title before producing a champion and a CC winner. Tipster of Exford, a son of Sniper of Exford, had little success in the show ring, but sired a CC winner. Rolf Peterson's Tuenga Kennel imported from both Denmark and Britain. The star of the kennel was Francehill Westaglow Benedict (by Ch. Sweetsultan of Shelert), who became a Norwegian and Danish champion.

The sadly missed Kari Schulstad, of the Ellingstone kennel, was a friend of many British breeders, and worked tirelessly for the betterment of the breed in Norway. Her imported Ellington Early Riser, a red sable by Ellington Express, became an International Champion, winning titles in Norway, Finland and Sweden. Early Riser left for Norway in whelp to the Davies's Ludjenka Lochinvar, a great favourite of mine that I thought unlucky not to have a much more successful show career. A dog from the resulting litter gained his Norwegian crown. Mrs Fishpool's Ellington kennel sold Kari Ch. Ellington Endless Folly (a granddaughter of Ch. Greenscrees Swordsman), who won further titles in Norway, Sweden and Denmark before producing a champion and a CC winner for Kari. Ellington Exploder, another son of Ellington Express, was imported and became a Nordic Champion. Kari then turned to Bill and Rita Henry's Greenscrees kennel, and imported Ch. Greenscrees Heidi Girl (a daughter of Ch. Greenscrees Swordsman), who was crowned in Norway and Sweden.

During the early 1970s many new kennels were founded in Norway, but use was made of the dogs already mentioned, so few were imported. One exception was Midnightsun Talk Of The Town, who was imported in 1974 and became the top producer of the time,

Lysebourne Double Up was astutely acquired by the emerging, and soon to become hugely successful, Leeland kennel of Aud Jorun and Helge Lie. Double Up's sire was Ch. Mistmere Marching Orders, whose immense contribution to the breed in Britain is described above, and Double Up also became a most influential sire. Influential British imports in the late 1970s included Sovereign of Monkreddan (by Ch. Jefsfire Freelancer) and Harribrae Harvester, a son of Monkreddan Psalm. They were both extremely unfortunate to miss their titles. Monreddan Superboy was luckier, as was Craytarn Lady's Double, the foundation bitch of the Tim-Tim kennel. She was sired in England by Double Up before he went to Norway.

The Lies later imported several bitches; all became champions or international champions. They included the Sumburgh bitches Lulubelle and Witch Hazel (both by Ch. Sumburgh Tesoro Zhivago) and the impeccably bred Riverhill Ring of Bells, by Ch. Riverhill Raider out of Ch. Riverhill Ring The Bell. The dogs Liberty of Lysebourne (by Kyleburn Gay Gordon) and Heathlow Martext of Lythwood (by Heathlow

Sunburgh Marcus) were also bought, and became titleholders and sires of champions.

The Sheltiestar kennel of Berit and Bjorn Johanson imported Lythwood Summertime, Ch. Shamaur Such A Night, and Morgana of Moldeva. All three gained titles and bred on. Philhope Sugar Sweet, by Ch. Rhinog The Gay Lancer, just failed to win her crown, but founded the Canyon kennel of Inger and Jan Nyberg.

Anne Karin Scheen combined with Astrid and Bjorn Thorstensen to import Morant Blue Belle of Shelridge, by Shelridge Gatecrasher, who gained her title and became the foundation bitch for Anne Karin's Miss Arin Kennel. Erna and Kjell Brevik bought Myriehewe Spanish Prince and Myriehewe Festivity from the Beaden sisters, and both achieved successes in the show ring.

In the 1980s there were significant improvements in homebred stock, which was enhanced by carefully chosen imports. Mondurles Bannoch, by Ch. Francehill Andy Pandy, became an International Champion for the Lies and sired an amazing twenty-two champions and twenty-eight CC winners. I cannot think of another dog of any breed with such a record.

The Lies also imported Bananarama of Kyleburn, a tricolour dog who gained his title and sired six champions, and Stationhill Speculator (a son of Scylla So Blessed at Felthorn). He too gained his title, and to date has sired ten champions and ten CC winners.

Norma and Sven Rognoy persuaded Patti and me to let two Haytimer sons, Philhope Shoestring and Franwick Saracen at Hartmere, to go to Norway (or become Vikings, as we liked to put it) after their successful puppy careers in Britain. Both became champions, and Saracen became an international champion. Shoestring had sired Ch. Franwick Sister Jane in his only litter in England, and in Norway sired two champions and eight CC winners. Saracen sired two champions and nine CC winners.

Other imports who made their mark in the show ring and as producers during this period are Schmoon Sportsman (by Ch. Marksman of Ellendale), Willow Tarn Touch and Go (by Willow Tarn Trueman), Skerrywood Black Chance (by Skerrywood Suede in Black), Rockaround Dusk at Shelridge (by Ch. Scylla Apollonia), and the bitches Bridgedale Golden Brocade (by Haytimer), Mountains Bella (by Tobormory of Willow Tarn), Lythwood Samba (by Ch Lythwood Spruce), and Shelridge Crystal Gazer (by Felthorn Ferryman).

In the 1990s there were further imports from England, and more than ten Norwegian-owned CC winners were bred by Birgitta and

Per Svarstaad in Sweden. The Leeland kennel imported Forestland Herald (by Glenmist Future Vision), Marklin Wild Jazz (by Ch. Marklin Espree), and Kindergate the Joker (by Kindergate MacDuffle). All three imports gained their titles and produced champions and CC winners.

Denmark

Captain Hauffmann, the founder of Shepherds Shelties in Sweden, introduced the breed to Denmark when he showed four Shelties at Copenhagen in 1934. Shepherds Butterfly, a sable daughter of S. Ch. Connis of Redbraes and Larkbeare Apricot Flan, was awarded the bitch CC, and his imported sable Netherkeir Chief won the dog CC. Further visits to Copenhagen in the next two years saw the same pair become the first Danish champion Shetland Sheepdogs, although there were no other Shelties in Denmark at that time. Denmark had no resident Shelties until 1948, when Ebba Aalegaard imported the bitch Miss Minny Morothy av Christensen from Sweden. A dog also came with Miss Minny, but grew much too large, so plans to mate the two imports were abandoned. Instead Miss Minny was mated in the same year to the Swedish dog Stormkappens Bar None, and produced a singleton, Spar-To Anjalille, the first Danish bred Sheltie.

Later in 1948, Ebba Aalgaard imported, from England, Hallinwood Warden and Hallinwood Gillyflower. Both were adults, and the latter was in whelp to Ch. Fydell Round-Up. Gillyflower won her Danish title, and two puppies from the mating to Round-Up became the first Danish-bred champions, Spar-To Bronze Badge and Spar-To Ballerina.

In 1949, Mrs. Christine Pederson moved from Sweden to Denmark with her mainly tricolour Pommery kennel. A blue-merle litter was born in 1951 at the Muchard kennel, to Shelties imported from Sweden.

The breed has developed in Denmark through relatively few, but carefully chosen and fortunate, imports. Int. Dan. N. Ch. Gay Monarch of Glenmist, a tricolour son of Ch. Riverhill Raider and Ch. Gypsy Star of Glenmist, proved to be a very influential sire, especially in the development of the Danish blue merles. The pure for sable Int. Dan. Ch. Jefsfire Allanvail Gold Spark, a Freelancer son imported at four years of age, was similarly influential on the sable lines.

In 1970, Kirsten and Bent Nielson imported to their Zobella kennel the tricolour Allanvail Midnight Express, who has arguably been the most influential stud-dog in Denmark. The high quality of his progeny was such that several of his sons gained their titles before he did.

Other imports of distinction were Dan. Ch. Riverhill Richness (by Ch. Midas of Shelert out of Ch. Riverhill Rare Gold), imported by Ebba Aalgaard, and Dan. Ch. Glyntirion Wee Laird of Marl (by Ch. Helensdale Ace out of Duskie Maid of Marl), who had won a Reserve CC in England and was bought by the Lukare kennel of Ludvig and Karen Redder. Dan. Ch. Elona av Sano, a blue merle Swedish-born bitch was bought by Ebba Aalgaard, and is in the pedigrees of many of today's blues. In 1973 the Poulsgaard kennel imported the blue merle dog, Dan. Ch. Tavena's Blue Pimms (by Ch. Loughrigg Kings Minstrel out of Dilhorne Blue Folly), who also had an impact on the development of merles in Denmark.

Sweden has provided many more dogs for Denmark than any other country, but only four of them have gained their titles in their adopted land. They are Elona av Sano, Smedjenas Jill, and the two Moorwoods, Wild Knight and Krystal Rose. Wild Knight is owned by Bianca Rosenkilde, whose English-based Zarvo kennel was the first to bring Shelties from America to Denmark in 1990; others have since followed.

Holland and Germany

The Second World War prevented any extensive development of the Sheltie in Europe, and great credit is due to these countries for the progress made in a relatively short time. Dutch breeders have made good use of imports from Willow Tarn, Shelridge, Milesend and Jefsfire, and German breeders have been equally successful with imports from Snabswood, Exbury and Ceirrhig.

Australia

The Sheltie arrived in Australia in 1936, when Mrs Esler imported Claudus of Camelaird and the tricolour bitch Riverhill Regal. Unfortunately, Claudus died young, and the Second World War prevented further imports. The foundation of the breed was delayed until the 1950s, when Mr F. Taylor imported Hallinwoods the Eagle Feather and Golden Fern, followed in 1958–9 by Supitor and Soldanella of Shelert, who both became Australian Champions.

Before the Shelerts arrived, a number of Shelties had been obtained from the New Zealand-based Riverbank kennel, and many currently successful Australian kennels can trace their pedigrees back to River-bank bitches mated to Supitor or his sire Eng. Ch. Starlight of Callart, imported one year later. The mating of Supitor to his daughter produced the outstanding Austral. Ch. Dundraroch Laird Donald and his brother Austral. Ch. Dundraroch Sunny Boy, credited with improving temperament.

In the 1960s Rodanieh Rock Mundi, Blazon of Callart and Ronanieh Francehill Typhoon were imported. All gained their titles and, together with Starlight, they are behind most present-day dogs in the state of Victoria. Austral. Ch. Rodanieh Francehill Typhoon mated another import, Austral. Ch. Kendoral Nymph, to produce the outstandingly successful Austral. Ch. Heatherburn Ace. Despite the reluctance of his owner to place him at public stud, Heatherburn Ace was highly influential on the breed in Australia. His sons the litter brothers Sheltiehaven Jody and Pancho had glittering careers, as did the same kennel's Austral. Ch. Sheltiehaven Rocket and Austral. Ch. Goldhaven Amazon Ace. Another son, Austral. Ch. Kerondi Othello, proved to be a potent stud force, and the three Nigma champion bitches, Qaiyara, Josephine and Nova Scotia, each produced CC winners by Ace.

A contemporary of Heatherburn Ace, Austral. Ch. Almaroy All The Way, was also a big winner, but was a half-hearted and little-used stud. His line still continues, though, through a tricolour son Austral. Ch. Areton Othello.

In the mid-1960s, the successful English breeder-exhibitor John Wayte emigrated to Australia with his family, taking Eng. Ch. Francehill Light Fantastic and her daughter (by Ch. Trumpeter of Tooneytown) Lisronagh Star. Both won their titles, and Star's daughter by her half-brother Blazon became Austral. Ch. Lizronagh Can Can, to whom many top-winning Shelties of New South Wales are traceable.

Barbara and Jeff Phillips imported. Eng. Ch. Happy Song of Tooneytown to their Nigma kennel. She was in whelp to Riverhill Rolling Home, and five puppies were born within thirty-six hours of her arrival, which was alarmingly delayed by the Suez crisis. Over a five-year period, Happy Song won her title, and her daughters and granddaughters won nine out of the ten CCs awarded at the Adelaide and Melbourne Royal Shows. The top-winning bitch Austral. Ch. Nigma Allegretta was a double granddaughter.

In 1968 of Ch. Riverhill Rampion, brought much-needed new blood lines to Australia. A record thirty-four champions resulted from the 150 litters he sired in a nine-year stud career, and he also won his Australian title.

The arrival in the late 1970s of Eng. Ch. Selskars Cloudberry of Greensands gave a much-needed boost to the breeding of blue merles, which are currently very strong in Australia. The import of Snabswood Sandbagger, a reserve CC and Junior Warrant winner in England, was mated with the bitch Yewdale Gypsy Rose producing the influential Austral. Ch. Nigma Nobel.

Another hugely influential sire was Austral. Ch. Daestar Dannaher, from the consistent kennel of John and Rae Davies. The tricolour import Austral. Ch. Felthorn Harvest Moon brought show ring success for John and Leslie Tanks, and he also sired winners. Other successful kennels include the Hillacre Shelties of Glenys and Norma Acreman, the Long family's Peerilees and the Kimbush Shelties. A relatively new generation of kennels, too numerous to mention, ensures the continuing quality of Australian Shelties.

South Africa

South Africa has a nucleus of dedicated breeders, whose dogs seem to relish the climate. As in Australia, the vast distances between the major cities make using stud-dogs and showing difficult, but have not stopped the development of the breed.

Several years ago, two of Britain's successful post-war breeder-exhibitors, Maurice and Sheila Baker, went to South Africa on a judging trip, and returned there to live, taking with them a small number of their Shelties. Success came immediately with Shemaur Tuesday Child, born in Britain, who gained her South African title, and SA Ch. Koihai Make A Wish of Shemaur. They imported Austral. Ch. Shelbrae Singing the Blues at Shemaur, who also became a South African champion.

The Grandgables kennel of Guy Jeavons has turned out numerous winners, including SA Ch. Grandgables Hot Off The Press, SA & Zim. Ch. Greenan Freebooter For Grandgables (imported from Britain), SA, Austral. & Zim. Ch. Beauideal Applause for Grandgables (imported from Australia), SA Ch. Kirrimist Frosted Lace for Grandgables, and Int. Neth. & SA Ch. Guarani de Caumerhof for Grandgables. A judging trip to Britain resulted in Guy and his partner Mark taking Milesend Dancing Major to South Africa. This CC-winning sable dog is believed to be genetically clear of CEA – a more than useful addition to the limited bloodlines in South Africa.

2

The Breed Standards

The current UK Breed Standard for the Shetland Sheepdog was agreed and adopted by the Kennel Club in 1986, and it is the sixth standard since the breed was granted official recognition. The first revision changed the height for dogs and bitches, but all revisions since have merely simplified or extended the original Standard's descriptions of the various points.

The opinions of the British breed clubs were sought when the Kennel Club instigated changes for the standards of all breeds in an attempt to make formats uniform. The aim was to produce a standard that was accurate and easily understood. After much soul searching and discussion, one or two minor changes to the standard for the Shetland Sheepdog were thought necessary, and the major difference from the Sheltie's previous standards was the deletion of the prominent list of faults. The purpose of this deletion was to encourage judges to recognize the virtues of the dogs rather than concentrate on the faults, and it ought also to encourage breeders to think positively about breeding in the desired virtues, rather than avoiding at all costs the faults.

The new standard's lack of a list of faults initially raised concerns that breeders and judges would forget about the faults to be avoided. Time has proved such fears largely groundless, although the apparent ease with which some judges seem to be able to overlook serious faults does sometimes make me wonder whether greater compromise would not have been better.

The Kennel Club Standard is recognized by breeders and judges in all countries that have a reciprocal agreement with the Kennel Club and the Fédération Cynologique Internationale (FCI).

In 1989 the English Shetland Sheepdog Club (ESSC) published an extended version of the Kennel Club Breed Standard: after each section of the KC Standard was added a fuller description or definition of the points, giving breeders and judges such a clear word-picture of the ideal Sheltie that no one can claim ignorance of what is required. The Club's additions are reproduced here separately, after the KC

Standard; but they should be read, as intended, in conjunction with the UK Breed Standard as a commentary on the various points.

The UK Breed Standard
(Reproduced by courtesy of the Kennel Club)

General Appearance

Small, long-haired, working dog of great beauty, free from cloddiness and coarseness. Outline symmetrical, so that no part appears out of proportion to the whole. Abundant coat, mane and frill, shapeliness of head and sweetness of expression combine to present the ideal.

Characteristics

Alert, gentle, intelligent, strong and active.

Temperament

Affectionate and responsive to his owner, reserved towards strangers, never nervous.

Head and Skull

Head refined; when viewed from top or side a long, blunt wedge, tapering from ear to nose. Width of skull in proportion to length of skull and muzzle. Whole to be considered in connection with the size of the dog. Skull flat, moderately wide between the ears, with no prominence of occipital bone. Cheeks flat, merging smoothly into well-rounded muzzle. Skull and muzzle of equal length, dividing point inner corner of eye. Topline of skull parallel to topline of muzzle, with slight but definite stop. Nose, lips and eye rims black. The characteristic expression is obtained by the perfect balance and combination of skull and foreface, shape, colour and placement of eyes, correct position and carriage of ears.

Mouth

Jaws level, clean, strong with a well-developed underjaw. Lips tight. Teeth sound with a perfect, regular and complete scissor bite, i.e. upper teeth closely overlapping the lower teeth and set square to the jaws. A full complement of 42 properly placed teeth highly desired.

Eyes

Medium size, obliquely set, almond shape. Dark brown except in the case of merles, where one or both may be blue or blue flecked.

Ears

Small, moderately wide at base, placed fairly close together on top of skull. In repose, thrown back; when alert brought forward and carried semi-erect with tips falling forward.

Neck

Muscular, well arched, of sufficient length to carry the head proudly.

Forequarters

Shoulders very well laid back. At the withers separated only by the vertebrae, but blades sloping outwards to accommodate desired spring of ribs. Shoulder joint well angled. Upper arm and shoulder blade approximately equal in length. Elbow equidistant from ground and withers. Forelegs straight when viewed from front, muscular and clean with strong bone. Pasterns strong and flexible.

Body

Slightly longer from point of shoulder to bottom of croup than height at withers. Chest deep, reaching to point of elbow. Ribs well sprung, tapering at lower half to allow free play of forelegs and shoulders. Back level, with graceful sweep over loins: croup slopes gradually to rear.

Hindquarters

Thigh broad and muscular, thighbones set into pelvis at right angles. Stifle joint has distinct angle, hock joint clean cut, angular, well let down with strong bone. Hocks straight when viewed from behind.

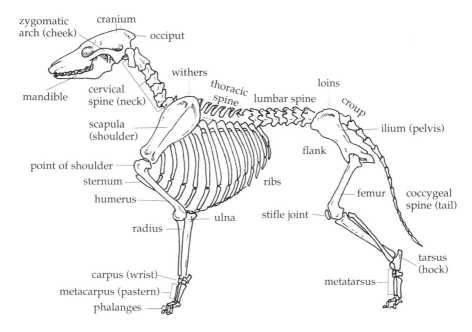

The points of the skeleton.

Feet

Oval, soles well padded, toes arched and close together.

Tail

Set low, tapering bone reaches to at least hock; with abundant hair and slight upward sweep. May be slightly raised when moving but never over level of back. Never kinked.

Gait/Movement

Lithe, smooth and graceful with drive from hindquarters, covering the maximum amount of ground with the minimum of effort. Pacing, plaiting, rolling or stiff stilted up and down movement highly undesirable.

Coat

Double, outer coat of long hair, harsh textured and straight. Undercoat soft, short and close. Mane and frill very abundant, forelegs well

51

feathered. Hindlegs above hocks profusely covered with hair, below hocks fairly smooth. Face smooth. Smooth coated specimens highly undesirable.

Colour

Sables Clear or shaded, any colour from pale gold to deep mahogany, in its shade, rich in tone. Wolf sable and grey undesirable.

Tricolours Intense black on body, rich tan markings preferred.

Blue Merles Clear, silvery blue, splashed and marbled with black. Rich tan markings preferred but absence not penalised. Heavy black markings, slate or rusty tinge in either top or undercoat highly undesirable; general effect must be blue.

Black & White and Black & Tan are also recognised colours. White markings may appear (except on black and tan) in blaze, collar and chest, frill, legs and tip of tail. All or some white markings are preferred (except on black and tan) but absence of these markings not to be penalised. Patches of white on body highly undesirable.

Size

Ideal height at withers: Dogs 37cm (14½in); Bitches 35.5cm (14in). More than 2.5cm (1in) above or below these heights highly undesirable.

Faults

Any departure from the foregoing points should be considered a fault and the seriousness with which the fault should be regarded should be in exact proportion to its degree.

Note

Male animals should have two apparently normal testicles fully descended into the scrotum.

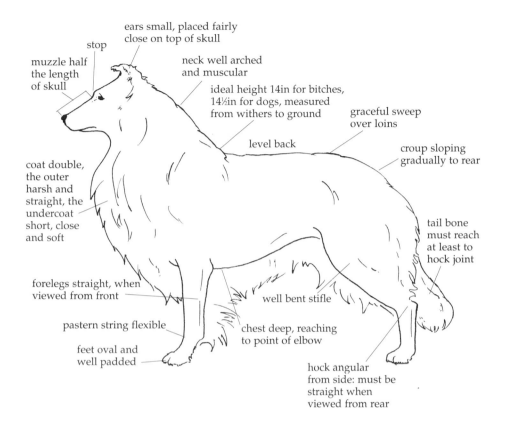

ears small, placed fairly
close on top of skull

stop

muzzle half
the length
of skull

neck well arched
and muscular

ideal height 14in for bitches,
14½in for dogs, measured
from withers to ground

graceful sweep
over loins

level back

croup sloping
gradually to rear

coat double,
the outer
harsh and
straight, the
undercoat
short, close
and soft

tail bone
must reach
at least to
hock joint

forelegs straight, when
viewed from front

well bent stifle

pastern string flexible

chest deep, reaching
to point of elbow

feet oval and
well padded

hock angular
from side: must be
straight when
viewed from rear

The main points of the Standard illustrated.

ESSC Extended Standard
(Reproduced by courtesy of the English Shetland Sheepdog Club)

General Appearance

A combination of the first sentence of this heading with phrases taken
from later paragraphs would read 'small, longhaired, working dog of
great beauty; strong and active but lithe and graceful, free from cloddiness and coarseness'. This would complete a picture of substance
and refinement in perfect balance. The dog of course should always
appear masculine and the bitch feminine.

53

Characteristics and Temperament

It will be helpful to read these two paragraphs in conjunction with one another. The resultant combination of qualities explains why, given sensible rearing, the Shetland Sheepdog makes an ideal family dog, and why, with sympathetic training, he shows such a marked aptitude for Obedience and Trials work.

Head and Skull

The character, quality and individual breed type of many dogs is expressed most eloquently in the head properties, and this is certainly true of the Sheltie.

Continuing the suggestion of symmetry which permeates the breed standard, the head must be balanced and in proportion to the individual dog. It must be refined, but not too fine, and the required wedge-shape, though comparatively long, should be blunt when seen (it must be noted) from the top or from the side.

The Standard lists quite accurately all the individual qualities which contribute to the perfectly balanced head, and although it does not appear in the official requirements, the term 'one-piece head' suggests the smooth moulding which enables the flat skull, the flat cheeks and the ideal stop to blend with the rounded foreface into a harmonious whole.

Seen from the side, the flat skull (not too frequently seen) should be absolutely parallel with the topline of the muzzle, but the skull must be on a very slightly higher plane because of the slight rise of the stop. Although slight, the outline of the stop is of course accentuated by the eyebrows. If the stop is too pronounced, the head frequently appears 'old fashioned' because a deep stop often seems to accompany a broad skull and possibly a dished face (in which the muzzle is slightly higher at the nose than in front of the eyes).

If the stop is too slight, the space between the eyes will be filled in, giving a decidedly 'foreign' look to the profile and the expression. The skull may appear to recede, and in some cases actually does so, a grave fault.

If the stop is too gradual, starting to rise well in front of the eyes, it will probably spoil the profile of the muzzle which, instead of being perfectly smooth and level throughout its length, may show a dip followed by a gradual slope towards the eyes. In this case too, the space between the eyes will probably be too filled.

correct outline of head
showing skull and
muzzle of equal length
and parallel planes

rounded skull

receding skull

drooping nose

total absence of stop
(straight through head)

Head outline.

two-piece head; stop too
deep and dish faced

So too little, too much or an incorrectly placed stop can alter the profile of the head and the expression quite drastically. This applies also to any lumps on the muzzle profile, any dip or droop of the nose-tip, or any bumps on the skull. Any deviation from the smooth parallel lines detracts greatly from the type and quality of the profile.

Since the underline of the muzzle when seen from the side must also suggest a blunt wedge, there should not be too much depth from the eye down through the back of the jaw, and the underjaw should be reasonably well developed. If the depth is too great and the underjaw weak, the effect will be sharply triangular rather than a blunt wedge.

As the Standard clearly states, the head should be in proportion to the size of the dog.

Mouth

The well-developed underjaw, besides completing the wedge, is usually associated with the desired tight lip formation. A weak underjaw, possibly accompanied by an inadequate lip formation, tends to reveal the incisors, especially when the dog's head is raised. This is an unsightly fault.

The markedly overshot jaw (mercifully seldom seen) can go with an over-long muzzle, possibly with a tendency to a Roman nose – a very bad and very ugly fault.

A level bite causes undue wear on the incisors.

An overshot jaw is a very rare (and serious) fault in a Sheltie, but individually misplaced lower incisors are sometimes seen and are certainly not desired. Misplaced canines are a very serious fault from both the functional and the aesthetic point of view.

Dentition faults (or omissions) appear to be hereditary to some extent, and although few Sheltie judges are likely to be too censorious over a single missing tooth or one very slightly misplaced incisor, breeding plans should not ignore the desirability of complete dentition.

Eyes

The correct eye is adequately described here, but its shape and placement make such a vital contribution to the typical expression that its importance cannot be over-emphasized. It is also the ideal complement to the wedge-shaped head into which it fits as though streamlined into position.

A large round eye on the other hand does not fit the shape of the head and gives a decidedly faulty expression. Because in the past this type of eye was a common problem, there has been a tendency for a 'nice small eye' to be regarded as desirable.

This is certainly not the case. A really small eye can give a very hard expression as can a black or light brown eye as opposed to a dark brown one.

The permitted range of eye colour in the blue merle Sheltie is quite wide. One or both eyes may be dark brown, blue or a combination of blue and brown. The eyes do not have to 'match' in colour. Two very pale blue eyes can produce a somewhat staring look but are unlikely to be penalized unless the expression produced has an adverse effect on the general appearance. Two darker blue eyes on the other hand can contribute to a very pleasing expression. There is also the rare but beautiful 'merle eye' in merles, where the eye is brown with a blue fleck or patches of lights.

Any trace of blue in the dark brown eyes of sables or tricolours would be a serious fault.

Ears

These standard requirements are fairly explicit and it should be noted that the ears should be placed *fairly* close together on top of the skull. While low-set, obliquely carried ears are obviously ugly and faulty, ears that are placed *very* close together can give an uncharacteristically sharp expression. Shelties' ears are *not* required to be 'bang on top-practically touching' as sometimes described with misplaced enthusiasm.

In case a change of a single word in the Standard should cause uncertainty ('falling' has replaced 'dropping' forward), it should be mentioned that the ears should curve gently over rather than appearing to drop sharply from a crisp crease. The latter carriage is another feature likely to give a sharp terrier-like expression. The tips of the ears should point forward and not to the side of the head to make the skull look broad, and heavy ears detract from the desired expression.

The character and appeal of the breed, including its essential sweet yet gentle expression, are so dependent on the ideal combination of the eyes and ears with the head properties, that all the remarks appearing under these headings must really be read and considered as part of the whole.

Neck

Although quite adequately described, this feature needs special emphasis because it is currently too seldom seen. This is a great pity as besides contributing to the flowing outline and proud head carriage, a reachy, crested neck adds so greatly to the look of distinction which a really top-class Sheltie should possess.

It is also important because in a breed of normal construction such as this, adequate length of neck will generally accompany adequate length of body and reasonable shoulder angulation. Without all of these features, a Shetland is unlikely to be able to stride out with the necessary freedom.

Conversely, the short, thick neck, frequently combined with steep shoulders and insufficient length of body, gives a dumpy outline and restricted movement, neither of which can be described as graceful. It must be remembered that the full adult coat (more especially the mane of the male) tends to disguise the reach of neck, so a 'stuffy' necked puppy is most unlikely to grow into an adult with proud and impressive head carriage.

Forequarters

Some people profess to find shoulders difficult to assess, which is presumably the reason that the upright shoulder is a common and persistent fault. In fact the good shoulder is not difficult to recognize and should be apparent without the need to handle the dog. The poor shoulder is even easier to recognize as it is likely to produce glaringly obvious faults in both stance and movement.

The well-laid-back shoulder (scapula) descends diagonally from the well-defined wither to meet the upper arm (humerus) at what is generally called the 'point of shoulder'. The upper arm should then run back at an angle of about 90 degrees from the shoulder to the elbow. The elbow, it will be remembered, should be equidistant from both the withers and the ground. If all the lengths and angles are correct, the elbow will be placed approximately beneath well set back withers. The dog will then be standing with its legs well under it, with a well-developed forechest.

If the shoulder and/or upper arm are too steep, the withers will be scarcely discernible as the upper tip of the scapula will be obscured by the base of the neck. The legs may appear to be in a perpendicular line down from the ears to the ground and there will be no apparent

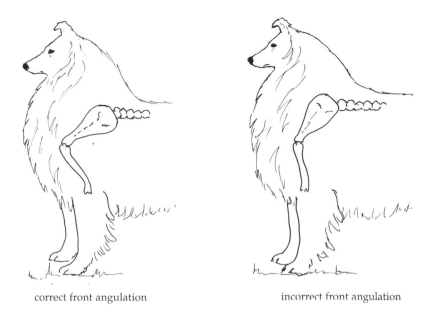

correct front angulation   incorrect front angulation

Front angulation.

forechest because the sternum (breastbone) will be obscured by the upper arm. The stride will be short and choppy and the forelegs may well be lifted too high. In fact the dog will look quite unbalanced in both stance and movement.

Now for the stipulation that the upper arm and shoulder blade should be approximately equal in length. The short upper arm is one of the faults most frequently criticized, but it may not be quite as common as suggested, if only because the term 'point of shoulder' is highly ambiguous. The shoulder assembly is really the combination of the shoulder blade (scapula) and the upper arm (humerus), which meet in a ball-and-socket joint. The tip of the humerus then continues to enclose and protrude slightly beyond the end of the scapula. So it is the upper arm, not the shoulder blade, which should be measured from this point. The end of the shoulder blade lies fractionally further back.

The foreleg is required to have 'strong' bone. This does not mean 'heavy' bone. The heavily boned foreleg will seldom accompany a flexible pastern, but it will all too frequently run straight down, with a 'thick ankle' instead of a flexible pastern, to a clumsy round foot. The

correct front   out at elbows   narrow front, weak pasterns

Stance: front view.

flexible pastern is vital as a shock absorber, but it must not be so sloping as to indicate weakness.

Body

This description of body corrects an error in the previous standard and
should be noted carefully. The measurement now given provides for a
body of medium length. It should not be too long in the back (i.e. from
the withers to the hips), as this would suggest a weak spine. The length
that gives strength is that measured from the point of really well angulated shoulders to the lowest point of a correctly sloping croup. This
construction allows scope for powerful hindquarters to achieve maximum propulsion and to combine with well-angulated forequarters to
provide the desired length of stride. A too-short body inhibits freedom
of movement and the flexibility required for turning at speed.

The depth of chest is often flattered by a profuse coat and should be
checked by touch when judging.

The level back (i.e. without dippiness) flowing into the graceful
sweep over the loins should not suggest a hint of roach, being simply
the fact that the Sheltie, as a galloping breed, should have strong, very
slightly arched loins, the 'graceful sweep' being enhanced by the
gradually sloping croup and low-set tail.

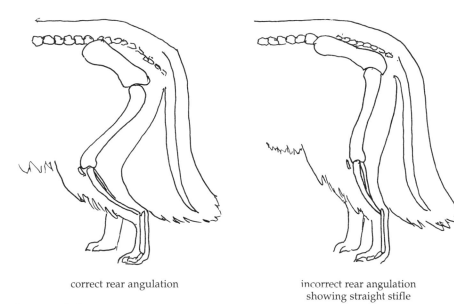

correct rear angulation

incorrect rear angulation
showing straight stifle

Rear angulation.

Hindquarters

The description of muscular, well-angulated hindquarters sweeping down to low set, well-angulated hocks suggests yet again the construction necessary to provide powerful, flexible propulsion at any speed. As with the steep shoulder or too short upper arm, lack of angulation or of adequate length of any of the bones of the hindquarters will give a short, stilted stride with too much up-and-down motion. To achieve rhythmic movement it is obvious that the construction of the fore and hindquarters must balance one another perfectly. The ideally angulated forehand cannot function adequately without the help of the well-exercised, normally developed muscles. On the other hand, muscles which are grossly over-developed in some specific area may be compensating for a fault of construction or an injury.

Feet

This is the ideal foot for the small, active dog required to move at speed on rough, rocky or slippery ground. The big, round foot (likely to accompany heavy bone) or the thin, flat, splayed foot (usually seen

correct rear stance   toeing out   cow hocks

Stance: rear view.

with thin, weak and spindly bone, sometimes the result of generations of poor rearing) are much less efficient as well as aesthetically unpleasing. Like the flexible pasterns, thick pads act as shock absorbers as well as protection, while strong, well-arched toes give grip when changing speed or direction.

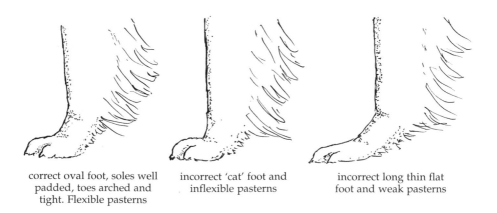

correct oval foot, soles well padded, toes arched and tight. Flexible pasterns   incorrect 'cat' foot and inflexible pasterns   incorrect long thin flat foot and weak pasterns

Feet.

Tail

This is self explanatory. A continuation of the spine, the long, gracefully carried tail completes the beautiful flowing outline.

The upward sweep (neither an acute twist nor a hook) may only be noticeable in movement. In the case of a too-short tail it may not be apparent even then, but the inert tail that hangs absolutely lifeless even when the dog is moving at speed is likely to have been injured or otherwise damaged.

The maximum height to which the tail may be raised when moving is a line which continues that of the back.

When the tail is checked for length, it should be also examined carefully in case it is kinked. Kinks are misplaced (sometimes accidentally displaced) vertebrae. Kinks can be situated anywhere along the tail, from the root to the tip. Occasionally puppies may be born with very short tails which are kinked in several places; this is not only most unsightly, but can also present practical problems, so kinked tails should be avoided at all costs.

Gait/Movement

Most aspects of correct and faulty movement have already been covered under 'forequarters' and 'hindquarters' so it will already be understood that the required long, smooth, effortless stride which only just clears the ground ('daisy-cutting action') is dependent largely upon the construction, angulation and, above all, the balance of fore and rear assembly.

If, for instance, the dog has a steep shoulder but well-angulated hindquarters, the forelegs will impede the potentially longer stride from behind. This may mean that the hindlegs may have to take evasive action in one of several different ways. Both hind feet may pass between the path of the forefeet causing the dog to move very close behind. Alternatively, the body may swing slightly sideways so that one foot may pass between and the other outside the track of the forefeet. If the forefeet are plaiting, the hind feet may need to pass outside the forefeet to one side, causing the bodyswing to be accentuated. Since the dog with steep shoulders may tend to raise the forefeet rather high in any event, this tendency will be exaggerated as it tries to remove the front feet as quickly as possible from the path of the rear feet. There are many variations on the theme of lack of balance between the forequarters and the hindquarters. All of them could result in ungainly and inefficient movement.

correct fast trot   hock joint too high   crossing over

correct slow trot   throwing hock joint out   cow hocks in action

Action: rear view

'Pacing' is, as often as not, a habit. It may be adopted by an obese or lazy dog or, as a result of faulty exercise on the lead. 'Road work' is only useful if the dog can be kept at a brisk trotting pace over a considerable distance. ('Pacing' occurs when the legs on the same side move in unison instead of, for example, front right leg, left back leg; this gives a rolling kind of movement.)

correct slow trot   too close   prancing movement

correct fast trot showing
single tracking   crossing over central
line of balance   too wide

Action: front view.

Other movement faults can result from the handler's bad habits. Dogs adapt themselves to the handler's pace and no dog is likely to move with a long smooth stride if its accompanying human is tripping along with a stiff, stilted, up-and-down movement!

Finally it should be explained that although the fact is not mentioned in the standard, the really well made Sheltie, like most other

correct movement at the
trot

faulty gait, showing dog
pacing – both feet on same
side move in unison

wrong, 'hackney'-like
action, due to insufficient
lay back of shoulder blade

Gaits: side view.

breeds of perfectly natural construction, uses the gait known as single-tracking in order to achieve the desired balance and economy of movement. Although in stance and at a walk the dog's legs remain perpendicular to the ground, as his speed increases, his legs begin to converge slightly until at a fast trot the inner edge of each foot would touch (but never cross) an imaginary central line.

Coat

This paragraph is self-explanatory. The correct double coat, with the furnishings as described, is one of the breed's chief beauties, while the texture offers maximum weather resistance. When a dog is in full coat it is virtually impervious to rain. The incorrect soft, fluffy coat, however, will absorb moisture like cotton wool.

Generally the male Sheltie will have a slightly more abundant and possibly harsher coat than the female, and he will have a more pronounced mane. The bitch will usually have more abundant petticoats and a more luxuriantly feathered tail. Despite its abundance, the coat should never appear to dominate the dog or obscure its outline. It must fit the body, showing off the graceful silhouette.

The so-called smooth coated specimen was fairly common during the breed's formative years but is never seen nowadays.

Colour

Little comment is required in the case of sables and tricolours except to point out the preferences for richness of tone and intensity of colour in the cases of the respective background colours, and the richness of tan markings in the case of tricolours.

In the case of blue merles the requirements are more specific so present more difficulties to the breeder and to the judge. Blue merles should be blue (not iron grey or mostly black!). As the Standard requires, the blue should be a clear silvery blue splashed or marbled with black. Large black patches are unattractive, as is a rusty tinge. A merle does not need to have tan markings but when these occur they should be rich, in which case they contribute à lot to the beauty of a good blue merle. Although colour in merles must always be an important factor, this must be taken into consideration with the whole dog. In tricolours, the black should be really black (not rusty or 'ticked' with white), and the tan rich, and the white really white.

Sables may be all colours from a very pale gold to a dark rich shaded sable, and all colours in-between. Wolf sables (where there is a greyish hue) are undesirable. So-called 'wheatens' (an extremely pale sable) are permissible.

Coloured ticking on white legs should not be penalised in any of the colours.

Quite understandably, most breeders and judges have their personal preferences as regards colour and (especially) white markings. The only real problem that may arise is if personal preference is allowed to become personal prejudice, and here judges must always be on their guard. However, there are always limits to which markings are acceptable from the point of view of general appearance. The Standard makes it clear that white patches (no matter how small) are not acceptable on the body (i.e. the trunk). A marking that disturbs the general effect of 'great beauty' can only be regarded as a handicap, but prejudices against, for example, a white blaze, a white strip up the stifle, a dark muzzle on a shaded sable or odd eyes in a merle, must be kept firmly under control when judging.

Size

The requirements here are precise, the only change being the fact that one-inch (2.5cm) under the ideal height is as undesirable as one inch over.

Faults

The Kennel Club's firm refusal to list specific faults under this heading is presumably a laudable effort to discourage so-called 'fault judging'. This is acceptable providing the aspiring judge or breeder remembers and applies the 'any departure' phrase.

To those who prefer a more positive attitude it is pointed out that any characteristic described as 'undesirable' may be fairly regarded as a 'fault', The 'highly undesirable' characteristic should be considered a serious fault.

Issued 20 April 1989

The American Shetland Sheepdog Association Standard, which was approved in 1959 and reformatted in 1990, is as follows.

The American Breed Standard

(Reproduced by courtesy of the American Kennel Club)

Preamble

The Shetland Sheepdog, like the Collie, traces to the Border Collie of Scotland which, transported to the Shetland Islands and crossed with small, intelligent, longhaired breeds, was reduced to miniature proportions.

Subsequently crosses were made from time to time with Collies. This breed now bears the same relationship in size and general appearance to the Rough Collie as the Shetland Pony does to some of the larger breeds of horses. Although the resemblance between the Shetland Sheepdog and the Rough Collie is marked, there are differences which must be noted,. The Shetland Sheepdog is a small, alert, rough-coated, longhaired working dog. He must be sound, agile and sturdy. The outline should be so symmetrical that no part appears out of proportion to the whole. Dogs should appear masculine; bitches feminine.

Size, Proportion, Substance

The Shetland Sheepdog should stand between 13 and 16 inches at the shoulder. *Note* height is determined by a line perpendicular to the ground from the top of the shoulder blades, the dog standing naturally, with forelegs parallel to line of measurement. *Disqualifications* Heights below or above the desired size range are to be disqualified from the show ring. In overall appearance, the body should appear moderately long as measured from shoulder joint to ischium (rearmost extremity of the pelvic bone), but this length is actually due to the proper angulation and breadth of the shoulder and hindquarters, as the back itself should appear comparatively short.

Head

The head should be refined and its shape, when viewed from top or side, should be a long, blunt wedge tapering slightly from ears to nose. **Expression** Contours and chiselling of the head, and shape and color of the eyes combine to produce expression. Normally the expression should be alert, gentle, intelligent and questioning. Toward strangers the eyes should show watchfulness and reserve, but no fear. **Eyes** Medium size with dark, almond-shaped rims, set somewhat obliquely in skull. Color must be dark, with blue or merle eyes permissible in blue merles only. *Faults* Light, round, large or too small. Prominent haws. **Ears** Small and flexible, placed high, carried three-fourths erect, with tips breaking forward. When in repose the ears fold lengthwise and are thrown back into the frill. *Faults* Set too low. Hound, prick, bat, twisted ears. Leathers too thick or too thin. **Skull and Muzzle** Top of skull should be flat, showing no prominence at nuchal crest (the top of the occiput). Cheeks should be flat and should merge smoothly into a well-rounded muzzle. Skull and muzzle should be of equal length, balance point being inner corner of eye. In profile the top line of skull should parallel the top line of muzzle, but on a slightly higher plane due to the presence of a slight but definite stop. Jaws clean and powerful. The deep, well-developed underjaw, rounded at chin, should extend to base of nostril. **Nose** must be black. **Lips** Tight. Upper and lower lips must meet and fit smoothly together all the way around. Teeth level and evenly spaced. Scissors bite. *Faults* Two-angled head. Too prominent stop, or no stop. Overfill below, between, or above eyes. Prominent nuchal crest. Domed skull. Prominent cheekbones. Snipy muzzle. Short, receding, or shallow underjaw, lacking breadth and depth. Overshot or undershot, missing or crooked teeth. Teeth visible when mouth is closed.

Neck, Topline, Body

Neck should be muscular, arched, and of sufficient length to carry the head proudly. *Faults* Too short and thick. **Back** should be level and strongly muscled. **Chest** should be deep, the brisket reaching to point of elbow. The ribs should be well sprung, but flattened at their lower half to allow free play of the foreleg and shoulder. Abdomen, moderately tucked up. *Faults* Back too long, too short, swayed or roached. Barrel ribs. Slab-side. Chest narrow and/or too shallow. There should be a slight arch at the loins, and the croup should slope gradually to the rear. The hipbone (pelvis) should be set at a 30-degree angle to the spine. *Faults* Croup higher than withers. Croup too straight or too steep. The **tail** should be sufficiently long so that when it is laid along the back edge of the hind legs the last vertebra will reach the hock joint. Carriage of the tail at rest is straight down or in a slight upward curve. When the dog is alert the tail is normally lifted, but it should not be curved forward over the back. *Faults* too short. Twisted at end.

Forequarters

From the withers, the shoulder blades should slope at a 45-degree angle forward and down to the shoulder joints. At the withers they are separated only by the vertebrae, but they must slope outward sufficiently to accommodate the desired spring of rib. The upper arm should join the shoulder blade at as nearly as possible a right angle. Elbow joint should be equidistant from the ground and from the withers. Forelegs straight viewed from all angles, muscular and clean, and of strong bone. Pasterns very strong, sinewy and flexible.

Dew-claws may be removed. *Faults* Insufficient angulation between the shoulder and upper arm. Upper arm too short. Lack of outward slope of shoulders. Loose shoulders. Turning in or out of elbows. Crooked legs. Light bone. **Feet** Should be oval and compact with the toes well arched and fitting tightly together. Pads deep and tough, nails hard and strong. *Faults* Feet turning in or out. Splay feet. Hare feet. Cat feet.

Hindquarters

The thigh should be broad and muscular. The thighbone should be set into the pelvis at a right angle corresponding to the angle of the shoulder blade and upper arm. Stifle bones join the thighbone and should be distinctly angled at the stifle joint. The overall length of the stifle should be at least equal the thighbone, and preferably should slightly exceed it. Hock joint should be clean-cut, angular, sinewy, with good bone and strong ligamentation. The hock (metatarsus) should be short and straight viewed from all angles. Dew-claws should be removed. *Faults* Narrow thighs. Cow-hocks. Hocks turning out. Poorly defined hock joint. **Feet** As in forequarters.

Coat

The coat should be double, the outer coat consisting of long, straight, harsh hair; the undercoat, short, furry, and so dense as to give the entire coat its 'stand off' quality. The hair on face, tips of ears and feet should be smooth. Mane and frill should be abundant, and particularly impressive in males. The forelegs well feathered, the hind legs heavily so, but smooth below the hock joint. Hair on tail profuse. *Note* Excess-hair on ears, feet, and on the hocks may be trimmed for the show ring. *Faults* Coat short or flat, in whole or in part; wavy, curly, soft or silky. Lack of undercoat. Smooth-coated specimens.

Color

Black, blue merle, and sable (ranging from golden through mahogany); marked with varying amounts of white and/or tan. *Faults* Rustiness in a black or a blue coat. Washed-out or degenerate colors, such as pale sable and faded blue. Self-color in the case of blue merle, that is, without any merling or mottling and generally appearing as a faded or diluted tri-color. Conspicuous white body spots. Specimens with more than 50 per cent white shall be so severely penalized as to effectively eliminate them from competition. *Disqualification* Brindle.

Gait

The trotting gait of the Shetland Sheepdog should denote effortless speed and smoothness. There should be no jerkiness, nor stiff, stilted, up-and-down movement. The drive should be from the rear, true and straight, dependent upon correct angulation, musculation, and ligamentation of the entire hindquarter, thus allowing the dog to reach well under his body with his hind foot and propel himself forward. Reach of stride of the foreleg is dependent upon correct angulation, musculation and ligamentation of the forequarters, together with width of chest and construction of rib cage. The foot should be lifted only enough to clear the ground as the leg swings forward. Viewed from the front, both forelegs and hindlegs should move forward almost perpendicular to ground at the walk, slanting a little inward at a slow trot, until at a swift trot the feet are brought so far inward toward centre line of body that the tracks left show two parallel lines of footprints actually touching a centre line at their inner edges. *There should be no crossing of the feet nor throwing of the weight from side to side.*

Faults Stiff, short steps, with a choppy, jerky movement. Mincing steps, with a hopping up and down, or a balancing of weight from side to side (often erroneously admired as a 'dancing gait' but permissible in young puppies). Lifting of front feet in hackney-like action, resulting in loss of speed and energy. Pacing gait.

Temperament

The Shetland Sheepdog is intensely loyal, affectionate, and responsive to his owner. However, he may be reserved toward strangers but not to the point of showing fear or cringing in the ring. *Faults* Shyness, timidity, or nervousness. Stubbornness, snappiness, or ill temper.

Scale of points

General appearance
Symmetry 10. Temperament 10. Coat 5.
Head
Skull and stop 5. Muzzle 5. Eyes, ears and expression 10.
Body
Neck and back 5. Chest, ribs and brisket 10. Loin, croup and tail 5.
Forequarters
Shoulder 10. Forelegs and feet 5.
Hindquarters
Hip, thigh and stifle 10. Hocks and feet 5.
Gait
Gait – smoothness and lack of wasted motion when trotting 5.
Total 100

Disqualifications

Heights below or above the desired size range, i.e. 13–16 inches. Brindle color.

Main Differences Between the Standards

Quickly scanning the American and English Standards gives the impression that they are very similar. Detailed study, however, reveals several fundamental differences in words, phrases, emphasis, and interpretation.

Arguably, the most important item in the standard of any pedigree dog is the General Appearance. The American Standard compares the relationship of size and general appearance between the Sheltie and the Rough Collie, to that between the Shetland pony and some of the larger breeds of horse. No such comparison appears in the English Standard. The Shetland pony is a strong, sturdy, cobby pony, with short, quite heavily boned legs, may resemble a scaled-down Shire horse, but bears no resemblance to the lighter, more elegant horses such as the Thoroughbred and the Arab, which perhaps offer a more useful comparison. Shelties should be represented as nimble, graceful and refined. The Shetland pony seems quite the wrong choice of horse to compare it to.

The American standard allows a dog to be a half-inch (1.25cm) bigger than the English Standard, and the impression that American

Shelties are 'much larger' than others may have more to do with the heavier bone and, despite similarity in the wording of the standards, the taper and depth of the head.

The description of the length of the stifle bone as equal to and preferably longer than the thighbone could also account for the greater hind angulation being greater than that of dogs bred and judged to the English Standard. Many other American-bred pedigree dogs also exhibit this characteristic.

The American system of judging by points is quite different from any of the methods used in Europe. As an international judge, used to the European systems, I would find it rather distracting to award marks for individual points of the Standard, and would be concerned that the best dog overall might not necessarily win under a point system of judging.

Despite common foundation stock and, for the most part, similarly worded standards, significant differences are extremely obvious between American Shelties and others. It is impossible to say why and how this came to pass, and it is to be regretted. There is a danger that as large numbers of American Shelties are available for export to other countries, the breed that is currently admired and loved in Europe and elsewhere could become a poor hybrid or the two different types, losing much of its elegance and sweetness of expression in the process. Conversely, few American enthusiasts would wish to exchange what they see as appealing and correct expressions and ideal substance for 'English'-type dogs, which some Americans have described as 'chicken boned, snipy and poorly coated'.

Is there a need or a desire to adopt one standard for the same breed of dog? Should there in fact be two separate breeds, as in the case of the Cocker Spaniel and the American Cocker, who also started as the same breed but became irreconcilably different? It is to be hoped that the outcome of the 1999 World Congress, hosted by the English Shetland Sheepdog Club for the discussion of such matters, will be to preserve the correct Sheltie type.

3

Choosing Your
Shetland Sheepdog

Why should you choose to own – or to put it more accurately, be owned – by a Shetland Sheepdog? Initially, you may have noticed a Sheltie out walking with his owner, or you may have a friend or relative who has one. You may have seen only a photograph in a book. Whatever, you will have been instantly attracted by the flowing, glamorous coat, and a sweet expression. If you have seen a Sheltie walking through a park with his owner, you may also have been impressed with the way it walked steadily, tail gently waving, looking endearingly up at his owner, with none of the straining at the leash you may have noticed in some other breeds.

It is unfortunate that some people think of the Sheltie as shy, almost to the point of nervousness, yappy, and even slyly aggressive. I have heard all these descriptions when out and about with our dogs. There is no denying that a very small number of Shelties display all of these undesirable characteristics, but they are not typical of the vast majority. A poor temperament is likely to be the product of the environment in which a Sheltie lives, or a result of inappropriate treatment.

The Shetland Sheepdog has inherited much of the robust good health that his ancestors needed merely to survive the hard life on the Shetland Islands. His outward appearance may have changed, but he has also retained much of the working ability of his forebears. Many Shelties compete at the highest level in obedience and agility competitions. They are willing to learn and eager to please, which means that they also integrate easily into whatever lifestyle and activities their owners decide for them.

Shelties can best be described as a one-family dog, rather than a one-man dog, although family friends who visit regularly are readily adopted into the circle of favoured people. This is not to say that Shelties do not like strangers, or that they are nervous of them, but a little reserve with newcomers is a trait found in many of the shepherding breeds. It usually takes the form of complete disdain, often to our acute

75

Greensands Gangsters Moll of Monkswood, bred by J. Edwards and owned by Mary Davies. (Photo. G. Russell.)

embarrassment. Having said this, I am sure there are many kennels and households no different from ours but that you'll be met by a pack of Shelties all anxious to claim you as a long-lost friend.

Although I have described Shelties as one-family rather than oneman dogs, they often chose for themselves, within the family one member with whom they will spend as much time as possible, often lying head on paws gazing steadily and adoringly at that person. Maddeningly, the object of this unswerving devotion can be the one person in the dog's life who neither feeds nor grooms him, nor even takes him for walks. If a Sheltie chooses you to be this special person he may display a tele-pathic ability to anticipate your thoughts and feelings, and react to intended commands before the words are uttered. Many owners say that their Shelties are uncannily aware that someone is approaching home long before the sound of a car engine or footsteps could possibly be heard. Devotion on this scale brings its own rewards, but as in all extremely close relationships, care should be taken to ensure that obsessive behaviour does not arise.

Finding a Puppy

Where should you buy one of these truly wondrous dogs? First, what not to do. Do not buy from a pet shop or large kennel that advertises many different breeds of dogs for sale. Puppies from these outlets are bred elsewhere by people unlikely to have the best interests of the breed at heart (and that also means your best interests). The puppies may have been bred in unsatisfactory homes, by people who have not even the most basic idea how to breed sound, healthy and typical dogs. Often the owners find themselves with a litter eating lots of food, and homes that were promised by acquaintances failing to materialize, so they sell the puppies as a job lot to unsavoury establishments.

Worse still, the puppies may have been born on one of the many accurately named 'puppy farms', where brood bitches are treated as puppy-manufacturing machines, and are bred from at every season, kept in pens like pigs. They are almost always mated to a dog on the premises who in all probability has nothing to commend his use as a stud, and the puppies are raised under a regime in which cost-effectiveness and profitability are the only considerations. Puppies born at these establishments, and there are very many such establishments, are collected by vans for the long journeys to kennels or pet shops, and are probably mixed with puppies from quite separate sources. The dealers supply a pedigree for each puppy sold, but you should not assume that this has any meaning whatsoever. I have seen many such pedigrees that are obviously invented, with dogs whose names are untraceable. Even kennel affixes that are not from Sheltie breeding kennels, but are well known in other breeds, have been noted.

Anyone buying from such an establishment should not be surprised if the unfortunate puppy grows into a poor specimen – assuming that the puppy does indeed grow up. Puppies bought in this way have not had the benefit of the correct and caring rearing practised by all dedicated specialist breeders, and may be quite unhealthy as a result. They sometimes have such severe health problems that even (invariably expensive) veterinary treatment fails to restore any meaningful quality of life.

You should also be cautious about advertisements for puppies in newspapers and other places. Some of them are perfectly genuine, and the puppies have been carefully reared and thoughtfully bred, but all too often puppies sold in this way are not, and prove to be a distressing and expensive disappointment.

It should be unnecessary to emphasize that the purchase of a puppy as a Christmas present is definitely not a good idea. Reputable breeders try to plan their litters so that puppies do not become available at this time. They naturally fear that the puppy will be rejected after the season of goodwill, and worry about the practical problems for a puppy trying to settle into a new home filled with exuberant revellers, or empty while his new owners attend parties elsewhere.

By far the safest way to buy a Sheltie puppy is to contact the Kennel Club and ask for the telephone number of the nearest breed club secretary. The secretary will be pleased to recommend a reputable breeder and exhibitor in your vicinity. If the recommended breeder has no puppies for sale, you will probably be given the name of another reputable breeder who is known to have puppies available.

Make an appointment to visit the breeder you select. Most breeders of repute are only too willing to show off their dogs to you, and you will be able to see and assess the relations of your prospective purchase. Be prepared for the breeder to ask you fairly searching questions about where you live, whether the puppy will be left alone for long periods during the day, whether your garden is securely fenced, and perhaps what experience you have with dogs. Do not be offended by this questioning: all reputable breeders who care for their dogs want to assure themselves that their puppies go to suitable homes. If the breeder does not know you, or if you have not been recommended by another breeder, do not be surprised if you are asked to provide a reference, to give assurance of your suitability. Many years ago, a lady travelled a great distance to see our puppies, and when questions like these were asked she replied, 'I have come, today, only to buy a puppy, not to adopt a child'. She drove the long distance home alone.

You may have questions of your own. Most breeders are prepared to list and discuss with prospective purchasers what they think are the major strengths and even faults of their dogs. On the other hand, they may not like persistent inquisition over minor faults of no consequence.

Look for breeders who are proud of their achievements, and enthusiastic about the breed in general, including dogs from other kennels. Beware of breeders who boast incessantly about their wins and their dogs, but have nothing good to say about anyone else's.

Steel yourself not to go against your better judgement. You may be unimpressed by the appearance or temperament of the dogs you see, or there may be some other reason why you would not feel comfortable buying a puppy from a particular breeder. If so, tell the breeder that you have other kennels to visit and that you will be in touch soon. Always, as a matter of courtesy, make contact again if only to say that you have purchased your puppy elsewhere.

It may be that a highly recommended breeder has no puppies available at the time of your visit, but has a litter due or planned in the near future. Puppies from breeders of high repute are always in more demand than those from other breeders, and you might have to ask for your name to be included on the list of people waiting for puppies. You will be contacted when one suitable for your requirements is available.

Ludjenka Lochinvar, owned and bred by Mr and Mrs R. Davies.

These are many decisions to make, and you may have to compromise or even change your mind completely. A good breeder will always try to provide you with what you want, but miracles are not possible. Breeders are regularly asked for a sable and white bitch (or tricolour or blue merle) 'with full white collar and full white legs, who will be exactly the correct size when adult, with perfect ear carriage,' and so on. When the enquirer is asked if the puppy is to be shown, the answer is almost always, 'No, I only want a pet.' The poor breeder has probably waited a lifetime for just such a bitch to come along!

Most caring breeders will not allow a puppy to go to a new home before it is eight weeks old. By that time, the breeder will be satisfied that the puppy is eating well and has no digestion problems, and that growth rate is satisfactory. Our puppies and those of many other breeders are born and raised in the house, and such puppies have been conditioned to the noises of vacuum cleaners and other domestic appliances, to ease the trauma involved in the dramatic change in environment. You may also find that puppies reared in this way are virtually house trained. Shelties are a naturally clean dog and it is never too early to encourage this tendency.

An Older Puppy or Dog

An eight-week-old Sheltie puppy is the most adorable, irresistible creature, but he is also completely time consuming and energy-sapping. If you do not feel able to undertake the exacting, though deeply satisfying, task of raising a puppy, investigate the alternatives. From time to time, an older puppy of six to eight months of age becomes available, because he has not fulfilled the promise he showed at eight weeks. Standards for the show ring are extremely high, and the puppy may be unsuitable for show only because of a very minor, cosmetic fault, which the breeder will clearly explain to you to ensure that you understand and are comfortable with the situation.

Vets and others sometimes warn that dire problems can arise with such puppies. Be cautious about accepting advice from non-specialists. If you are worried, contact the breeder. Any reputable breeder will be more than happy to discuss your concerns.

Kennels sometimes want a new home for an older bitch that has been bred from, or, if numbers are increasing beyond the kennel's capacity, perhaps a winning show dog. You might wonder if such dogs will settle into the home routine, or if they will pine for their original home and companions. There is no need to worry. Shelties are highly intelligent dogs, who very quickly realize the advantages of being the sole occupier of the fireside rug or easy chair, and the lone recipient of affection from a new food provider. If you are fortunate enough to secure such a dog, however, *do not* allow him to run free without collar and lead for at least one month, or as long as you feel he takes to accept you and your home. Too many tragedies have occurred with dogs bolting from new homes before they have settled in fully.

As I write this, we have just had a visit from a dog who went to his new home at slightly more than two years of age. He was clearly delighted to see us again, but was waiting at the door when his new owner prepared to leave, and preceded her down the drive without a backward glance. It is comforting to know that he settled so well, though I must admit to a slight feeling of betrayal!

Dog or Bitch

Many prospective owners assume that bitches are more affectionate than dogs. In fact male Shelties may be even more affectionate than females, whose behaviour and mood swings can alter with their reproductive cycles. Dogs are generally more consistent in behavioural patterns. Buyers also think that dogs will roam in search of bitches in season, while bitches will stay at home, but again this is not necessarily true. Sheltie males appear to have a weaker libido than males of many other breeds, in whom the search for a mate seems an overwhelming impulse. A Sheltie bitch, on the other hand, attempts the most daring of escapes in her search for a suitable Lothario at the peak of her season.

Sheltie bitches can have seasons every six months, and tend to lose their coats afterwards, so unless you intend to breed, a male may be the best choice of show dog as well as pet. Two disadvantages are that a male is far more likely than a bitch to scent mark when taken into a strange house and occasionally, one or both testicles fails to descend into the scrotum when the dog reaches maturity. This condition should not cause alarm unless you want to show him. They can be removed, but be cautious about seeking any operation that is not absolutely necessary.

Ch. Riverhill Ricotta, owned by Mrs Birtles.

If you dream of breeding your own show dogs eventually, purchase the best bitch available, rather than a dog. Unless your dog puppy grows into a superb specimen, winning consistently in the ring, he is unlikely to be an attractive proposition as a mate for any bitch you may later acquire. It is definitely worth remembering that the best sire in the country is available at the end of a car journey.

Collie Eye Anomaly

Since 1969, most breeders have had their dogs tested for the known condition of Collie Eye Anomaly, or CEA (*see* Chapter 8), and your breeder should be able to show you the relevant certificate for your puppy and other relations. If the puppy offered to you does not have a clear certificate and is only to be kept as a pet and not to be bred from, there is absolutely no reason for you to be concerned. CEA is a non-progressive condition that will not worsen with age and, providing that your puppy has not been diagnosed as having one of the more serious forms, he will not suffer any complications and will have the same vision as an unaffected puppy.

Choosing from a Litter

If a puppy is to be a companion only, and you have no intention to breed or to show, ensure that this is clearly understood when you first contact a breeder. A breeder must know your intentions in order to offer you a choice of puppies that are suitable for your requirements. Any puppies thought to show the promise of success in the show ring would not be offered to you if you wanted a puppy solely as a pet. If you make it clear you intend to show your puppy, no breeder of repute will offer you a dog with any obvious serious fault. Please remember, though, that the perfect Sheltie has yet to be bred. The Sale of Goods Act in Britain covers transactions that involve animals, and designed to protect the interests of the purchaser. Most unfairly, there is no guarantee that litigation brought against a breeder will be unsuccessful, even if the purchaser originally told the breeder that he wanted only a pet, but later decided to show and breed, and was then disappointed that the dog was not successful.

Presuming that there is a choice of puppies, be guided by the breeder, who should be able to anticipate fairly accurately how each puppy will look when adult. Colour and markings are very misleading at this age, and your breeder will explain that, although it is difficult to believe, the grey colouring of a particular puppy will change and become the most glorious fiery gold in adulthood. White markings, particularly those on the head, diminish as the puppy grows. Narrow white blazes tend to disappear completely, and full white collars have a disconcerting tendency to shrink to a narrow white line around the neck. The absence of luxuriant white markings is no indication of the relative merits of puppies. I am often reminded of a saying beloved of my grandfather, descended from generations of farmers, 'A good horse is never a bad colour'.

There is much folklore attached to choosing a puppy, most of which is utterly wrong. The notion that the smallest is the runt of the litter and will never make a good dog is completely without foundation. Often the smallest at eight weeks becomes the largest at adulthood. Choosing the one who comes to you first is said to ensure that your choice will be a friendly and outgoing adult, but a very extrovert puppy may in fact become an over-exuberant adult. The puppy who sits and calmly assesses you before coming to you, is likely to be an intelligent, well-adjusted companion when mature. A puppy who wants to run away, or shows obvious signs of distress at your presence, cannot be described as exhibiting normal behaviour, but with a patient and understanding upbringing he may be quite different as an adult.

Unless you are an experienced breeder-exhibitor, you will need the breeder's help if you wish to purchase a show prospect or foundation bitch. No reputable breeder wants to jeopardize a hard-won reputation by allowing a dog of inferior quality to appear in the show ring. Even so, there is no guarantee that a puppy identified as being 'promising' will fulfil your expectations. Sheltie puppies look very different from adult Shelties, and the changes in appearance as they grow are dramatic, particularly in the head. These and other things, such as entirety, and the placing and number of adult teeth, are unknown factors over which you have no control. It is not until puppies are over a year old that you can be confident that you will not be surprised and dismayed by some unforeseen development.

Colour and Markings

What singles out the potential champion from his littermates at eight weeks old? At first sight all puppies have instant appeal. If the breeder's line breeding theories have worked in practice, the puppies should bear more than just a passing resemblance to each other. In a litter that contains only sable-and-whites, the colour and markings may be completely different on each of the puppies, but markings should not be among your initial criteria unless mismarking is apparent (white markings on places other than specified in the Breed Standard). The black of a tricolour must be intense, and the tan markings rich rather than pale in hue, if your choice is to show the strong contrasts in colour that make tricolours so eye-catching when in full adult coat. In a blue merle puppy, the clear silvery blue required by the Breed Standard should be clearly apparent, and the marbling effect should be clearly defined and well distributed to ensure the correct coloration as an adult. This colour can be heartbreaking when puppies excel in other ways, but have sandy or grey background colour, or are too heavily splashed with black.

Shelridge Gatecrasher, owned and bred by Mrs C. Aaron. (Photo. D. Aaron.)

Conformation

When assessing the conformation of puppies, we find it much more informative to watch them at play in an open space, where they come to rest in a natural stance, rather than setting them up on a table and examining them. Under such examination, puppies can far too easily be apparently condensed or stretched into the shape you are hoping for. At eight weeks, we look for a square, rather than oblong, body shape, with a long reachy neck. The squarer puppy is more likely to have the correct height-to-length ratio as an adult, whereas the more oblong puppy may develop too much length for his height as an adult. An oblong shape is often a sign that a puppy will grow too big for the Standard.

The lay-back of the shoulder and the return of the upper arm can be clearly felt in the puppy, and are most easily assessed when the puppy is standing in a normal position of alertness, with the front feet well behind an imaginary line drawn perpendicularly down behind the ears. If the feet appear in front of that line, there is every chance that the puppy will have straight shoulders, or be too steep in the upper arm, or perhaps even have both of these serious faults. The forelegs of the puppy should be straight when looked at from a head-on position, and should be well boned. You must feel for the strength of bone, as fluffy fur on the legs of puppies can give an illusion of thickness.

At the rear of the puppy, the stifle joint should show good even angulation at this stage. A straight stifle on a puppy will not miraculously turn into a well-turned stifle on the adult. The hock should be vertical to the ground when the puppy stands at rest. Sickle hocks (hocks that slope inwards and under the body rather than appearing vertical) are a very ugly fault that is also apparent at this age. When viewed from the rear the hocks should turn neither inwards (cow hocks), nor outwards (barrel hocks). At the back end of the puppy, check that the tail reaches at least to the point of hock, and that it is set on low at the croup. The tail should be free from any kinks or twists (an undesirable legacy from our Spitz ancestry). A puppy whose tail does not reach the hock joint will probably be 'set on' too high. Often he will have too square an outline and as an adult will not show the delightful sweep over the loins.

Entirety

Checking an energetic eight-week-old puppy to see if he will become entire is very difficult. It is best to wait for him to become sleepy and relaxed before you feel for the two tiny lumps, hopefully in the scrotum but definitely in the lower groin. This is a skill that some breeders have developed more than others. However dexterous and sensitive your touch may be, there is no guarantee that two testicles found in this position will descend fully into the scrotum by the time your puppy is six months old, and cases of 'disappearing testicles' are well documented. I would think all Sheltie breeders have experienced the totally crushing disappointment of a cherished and long-planned dog puppy, virtually perfect in every other way, failing to become entire. After several of these harrowing, hair-greying experiences, many breeders vow never again to keep a dog puppy unless he is fully entire at eight weeks.

I find it extremely surprising that so many male puppies do in fact become entire, considering that quite a number of the most influential stud-dogs of the past were monorchid, and I wonder if the condition is inherited in the way we have been led to believe. Test matings in some other breeds lead to the conclusion that the sisters of monorchid dogs produce a significantly higher proportion of monorchid puppies than their affected brothers. Perhaps Sheltie-breeders have been holding the wrong gender responsible.

The Head

Anticipating entirety is difficult, but assessing head qualities in a youngster is a veritable minefield! I am convinced that some lines and families develop head characteristics at different times, but I am not at all certain that this accounts for the wide variation in head type seen in adult show classes. Instead, I have come to believe that the extremely mixed heritage of the Sheltie shows disproportionately more in the head and expression than anywhere else. This, coupled with the fact that it is so difficult to anticipate what physical changes will occur, lead to an acceptance level that is probably far lower than it should be.

Beware the puppy whose head is almost a perfect miniature of what is required in an adult. This characteristic often signifies that the dog will become too strong and coarse in the head, and may indeed grow too big. At this age a shorter, chunkier head is likely to be a better indication of correctness, but a head that is too short and chunky, and too deep, could become a short adult head with too deep a stop. Assessing heads is difficult even for those who have bred generations of correctly headed dogs, and some never master it.

I can only describe, inadequately I am sure, what we hope to see in the heads and expressions of our puppies. At eight weeks, the top of the skull should look extremely flat, and may recede slightly in relation to the line of the foreface. The stop should appear deep in proportion to the depth of the foreface, which we prefer to be relatively short and well rounded, with the underjaw particularly well developed and the lips fitting tightly together when looked at from the front. The deep stop means that the eyes are placed forward at this stage, but as the head grows into the blunt wedge shape of the adult, the eyes will become oblique, as they are required to be.

The shape of the eye should already be almond. A large round eye may improve a little with time, but is extremely unlikely to change enough to become the correct size and shape. It is so important to avoid large eyes that there is a danger of choosing eyes that are too small and beady. The temptation must be avoided at all costs, as this type of eye will always result in a small-eyed adult with a hard, mean and most untypical expression. The Breed Standard clearly requires a medium-sized eye. An incorrect eye completely alters the Sheltie expression.

Incorrect ears seem to nullify all the advantages of even the most exquisite eye. Ears that are very small and thin, even though they are adequately tipped, and very well placed already, are almost certain to cause problems when the puppy starts teething. Consider whether you want the stress of trying to ensure that your puppy's ears, which seem to have minds of their own, remain tipped. If you are offered a puppy that at eight weeks needs aids to attain the correct ear carriage, you can expect to have a continuing battle – and one that you may lose.

We like to see, at this age, a puppy whose ears are thickly coated with fur, placed fairly high on his head, facing forward rather than hanging down sideways, and falling forwards so that the ear tips touch the skull. There is still the possibility that extremely heavy and long ears will struggle to reach the correct carriage, but we feel that more effective help can be given to this sort of ear than to the thinly coated, smaller type of ear.

Coat

One of the principal glories of an adult Sheltie, and one that is rightly emphasized in the standard, is the long, flowing, glamorous coat. Correct coat – a soft furry undercoat and long harsh top coat – is definitely inherited, as is lack of coat length, but if you see the dam on your visit to choose a puppy, you may be forgiven the fleeting thought that your puppy will never grow a coat. Shelties are usually wonderful mothers who give everything to their litter. A dam may appear a little thin as a result, despite eating an astonishing volume of food. Her coat looks poor, and she loses all the hair under her tummy so that the puppies can reach the 'milk bar' without hindrance. She may also have had most of the long hair on her petticoats and tail removed by the breeder to avoid any problems during the actual whelping. Return to the kennel in six months' time to see the mother of your puppy looking her best again.

Ch. Myriehewe Witchcraft, bred by Miss G. Beaden and Mrs J. D. Clarke, and owned by Miss G. Beaden. (Photo. Garwood, by kind permission of Dog World.)

There is no hard and fast rule to adhere to when you are looking for a puppy that will grow the correct coat. I know many breeders who have sold a puppy not expecting it to have a good coat, only to be astounded on seeing it as an adult, with a huge coat practically trailing the floor. We look for a puppy whose coat is thick and dense and resembles that of a Persian kitten, with long, straight guard hairs showing through, and we have never been disappointed with such a coat when the puppy is fully grown. Some families, though, are noted for puppies that show much less fluffy undercoat, but whose long guard hairs appear more exaggerated. Both types of puppy coat indicate a correct adult coat, but as with all these features there is no guarantee.

Ch. Lythwood Skymaster, owned and bred by Mr D. Rigby.

Size

The influence on size of early known Collie crosses, and perhaps later ones, continues to haunt Sheltie breeders. Not too long ago, at the boarding kennel of a close friend, we saw an impeccably bred Sheltie that measured 24in (60cm) at the shoulder – nearly twice as tall as it should have been. Although far fewer oversize Shelties appear in the show ring today than in the past, predicting the height that a six- to eight-week-old puppy will reach is still anything but an exact science. It is a very brave, some might say foolhardy, breeder who states, categorically, that a puppy will finish growing at the correct size.

There are many theories on how best to estimate the eventual size, ranging from using your instinct as to whether the puppy looks the right size to recording the birth weight of the puppies and rejecting any that are more than whatever figure is thought to have produced the best results in previous litters. Some breeders have recorded weights weekly, over many years, plotting them on a graph, to give an indication of the eventual height. We have tried almost every conceivable method of calculation, and find that in our line, the most accurate forecasts occur when a six-week-old puppy weighs 3lb 8oz (1.6kg), and gains no more than 1lb 8oz (680g) by eight weeks. I must stress that although this appears to be a fairly accurate forecast for our line, the formula may not apply to dogs of different breeding.

A Look of Quality

In addition to all these physical attributes, you may see something impossible to define, a look of sheer quality that shines out of the truly outstanding puppy. Once seen it is never forgotten, and the sight of a youngster standing in just the same way as a long-gone relative, and looking at you with exactly the same enquiring expression, is a deeply emotional as well as exciting moment.

A New Puppy

Before you take your chosen puppy home, the breeder should give you the pedigree, together with the registration document. The breeder will have signed this for you to forward to the Kennel Club with the relevant fee, so that the puppy can be transferred to your ownership. A conscientious breeder also gives you a diet sheet to follow. We and many other breeders, as a matter of course, present new owners with a little parcel containing some of the food the puppy is used to, and a small piece of the blanket he has shared with the other puppies. We find that the smells on the blanket have a comforting effect during the first, possibly traumatic, days in a new home. The parcel also contains the tattered remnants of one of my old socks, which the puppies have played with together! Most breeders have arranged insurance cover for the next six weeks. Whether you continue with the policy after that is your decision.

We find it a terrific wrench letting our puppies go, and know that other breeders do too. If for any reason your circumstances change, and you are unable to care for your dog, a reputable breeder wants to be the first to know so that the dog's best interests are served. We do not forget our puppies and ask all purchasers to maintain contact and tell us first of any concerns they may have, or just keep us informed of the puppy's progress. Photographs inside Christmas cards are a particular source of pleasure.

A puppy can travel home on the lap of a passenger in a rear seat of the car. Put the puppy on a towel and take plenty of kitchen towel in case of messes. Shelties are usually very good travellers, but drive as smoothly as possible, just in case.

4

Puppy Management

Get everything ready for the new puppy before you bring him home. You need to make arrangements for feeding, sleeping and house-training. You should also ensure that your garden is escape-proof – Sheltie puppies can squeeze through tiny gaps and holes. It is wise to reinforce any existing fencing with 3ft (1m)-high chicken wire. Sink it 6in (15cm) into the ground, to prevent the puppy wriggling underneath, and staple the wire securely into place.

Bringing a New Puppy Home

Your puppy will not have been fed before the journey. When you arrive home, offer him some food, in case he is hungry, but do not try to make him eat – the journey and the change of surroundings may blunt his appetite for a while. The breeder will probably supply a diet sheet for the puppy, and you should follow this carefully. Ask for it in advance, so that you have the right food ready. Fresh drinking water should be available at all times, preferably in an earthenware or heavy metal bowl with a narrow top, so that the puppy cannot paddle in the water or tip the bowl over in play.

The puppy must have a bed of his own, but at this stage there is no point in buying a purpose-made dog bed. Wicker baskets, foam-filled beds and bean bags may look good, but puppies quickly destroy them, and may choke on the foam or bean-filling. It is better to provide a cardboard box turned on its side, with a piece of blanket to sleep on. You can replace the box if the puppy chews it to destruction, and invest in something more stylish when he has finished teething.

Keep play times brief to begin with. Your puppy has a lot to get used to, and will easily get tired. For the first day or two, you may want to cradle him all the time, but it is kinder to introduce him to his bed whenever he looks heavy-eyed. He is more likely to settle at night if he has become used to his bed during the day.

At Night

A puppy's first night in a new home is bound to be difficult. He misses his litter mates and his mother, and tells you so with plaintive howling. Do not be tempted to take him to your room: sharing a bed with a puppy is one thing, sharing it with an adult dog is quite another. Be strong and put up with a few nights of disturbance, or your puppy will quickly learn that your will weakens the more he complains. He may settle better if he has a small, loud, ticking clock under his blanket, and a well-wrapped hot water bottle to snuggle up to. The clock is said to simulate the heartbeat of his former littermates. He is unlikely to require either of these devices after a few days when his surroundings become more familiar. It also helps if the puppy's bed is in a secure enclosure, so that he cannot wander around in the night. You can improvise or buy puppy panels which clip together to make a pen. Put a large polythene sheet on the floor of the enclosure, and cover it with plenty of newspaper. Enclosing the dog's bed in this way helps him to learn to keep to his own area of the house. If you acquire your puppy during summer, remember to close the curtains in the room or he may wake at first light.

Monkswood Marauder (rear), and litter brother Ch. Monkswood Moss Trooper as puppies. (Photo. Richard Cobby.)

Ch. Mountmoor Blue Boy, bred by Mr and Mrs J. Ferguson, and owned by Mrs C. A. Ferguson and Mrs E. J. Ford.

Play

Play is essential for puppies, although you should take things gently for the first few days. It helps form the bond between puppy and owner, and is also important in developing a puppy's character. Sheltie puppies who have not had the benefit of play are unlikely to develop into well-adjusted adults, and lack the charm and personality that characterizes the breed. Pet stores sell a huge number of toys alleged-ly designed for dogs, but an alarming number of these are quite unsuit-able for a puppy. Choose toys made from hard rubber or nylon that they cannot tear to pieces, or knotted hide chews, as these cause no

95

(Above) *Callart The Dancing Flames, owned and bred by Miss Olwen Gwynne-Jones. (Photo. Jeff Phillips, Australia.)*

BEST PUPPY

Ch. Shelridge Sunflower, winning Best Puppy in Show at National Working Breeds, with Judge Mr Terry Thorn and owner/breeder Mrs Christine Aaron. (Photo. Dalton.)

Ch. Herds The Helmsman, joint breed-CC record-holder, owned and bred by Miss M. Gatherall. (Photo. Carol Ann Johnson.)

Ch. Myriehewe Rosa Bleu, joint breed-CC record-holder, owned and bred by Irene Beaden.

Ch. Tegwell Wild Ways at Sandwick, Top Stud-dog All Breeds 1997/98, owned by Mr C. Mayhewe and bred by Mrs J. Stanley.

(Below) *Consistent type: Milesend dogs owned by Mrs J. Miles. From left, Chelmarsh Countess at Milesend, Milesend Dancing Queen (one CC), Ch. Milesend Dancing Along, Ch. Milesend Smart Enough, Milesend Majestic, Milesend Morris Dancer, (Res. CC), Ch. Milesend Storm Warden, and Milesend Dancing Major (one CC).*

(Above) *Promising. The author's Ch. Hartmere Hallmarked at eight weeks.*

(Right) *Still promising at sixteen weeks.*

(Below) *Promise fulfilled. Ch. Hartmere Hallmarked at thirteen and a half months.*

Can. Ch. Kensil's Ice Dancing, bred and owned by David and Sylvia Calderwood. (Photo. Jan Haderlie.)

(Below) Int. Nord. Ch. Eastdale Classic Clown, successful show and stud-dog, owned and bred by Berit Book, Sweden.

Int. Ch. Starbelle Simply Splendid, cleverly named by owner/breeder Mudeleine Lund, Sweden.

Ch. Beckwith Bit of a Vagabond at Shelmyth, bred by Cath and Dave MacMillan, and owned by Mrs Roseanna Smith.

Harribrae Harrier, Reserve CC winner, owned and bred by Nan and Harry Wheeler.

(Below) Ch. Seavall Sheen, owned and bred by Elmer Robinson and Jill Hardman.

a small amount about four times a day. Their diet should include vitamins, minerals and trace elements in addition to proteins, fats and carbohydrates. Supplements are available, but too many can have a retarding effect on growth and development. A typical diet sheet for an eight-week-old puppy might be as follows:

Breakfast One wheat cereal bar and goat's milk mixed to a porridge-like consistency, served warm with a teaspoon of honey and a pinch of calcium and phosphate supplement.

Lunch Two heaped tablespoons of cooked minced meat or tinned puppy food mixed with an equal quantity of pre-soaked puppy-biscuit meal (pre-soaking is essential to stop the meal swelling in the puppy's stomach). Substitute fish or scrambled egg for the minced meat to give variety and stimulate the puppy's appetite.

Late afternoon Same as lunch.

Supper Same as breakfast, without the supplement.

There are also several varieties of complete dry food, which contain all the nutrients a puppy needs and are certainly very convenient. Give the amount recommended on the packet for your puppy's age and size, and always provide plenty of fresh water, as there is very little in the food itself. The manufacturers recommend that these foods should not be mixed with anything else, as this upsets the nutritional balance, so do not be tempted to add supplements as they may do more harm than good. Occasionally a puppy becomes bored if he is always offered the same food, especially if he is being reared on his own. If this happens, you might disregard the rules and stimulate his appetite by mixing the complete food with gravy.

The number of meals should gradually be reduced until the dog is eating only one (or perhaps two) meals a day. If the diet sheet does not indicate when and how to reduce the number of meals, ask advice from your puppy's breeder. Any changes to a puppy's diet should be very gradual. Mix small amounts of the new food into the usual meals, and increase them daily until the change is complete. Remember to increase the quantities of food given as the diet sheet recommends. Owners have been known to continue to feed puppies with the diet appropriate for an eight-week-old, and then wonder why they are not thriving at twelve weeks.

Some of the author's early champions. From left: *Ch. Hartmere Harris Tweed, Ch. Hartmere Heather, Ch. Philhope Stardust, Ch. Hebson Galeforce at Hartmere, Ch. Haytimer of Hanburyhill at Hartmere, and Ch. Rainelor Reinetta. (Photo. M. Hart.)*

Feeding Problems

A puppy may initially devour his food with relish and then suddenly become quite picky. A new owner is bound to be concerned at any loss of appetite, but try not to become over-anxious, as a puppy will sense your anxiety and may eat even less. Take the food away if the dog shows no interest in eating more after about ten minutes, and do not try feeding him again until the next meal. Dogs have different needs and appetites, and healthy dogs will eat when they are sufficiently hungry.

Sometimes puppies who have lost their appetite also suffer from diarrhoea. This is often due to overeating, perhaps because the owner is overfeeding, or because the puppy is used to competing for food with brothers and sisters. Another cause could be an intolerance of cow's milk, which would after all not have formed part of the diet of the dog's wild ancestors. It may help to use goat's milk, which is closer to a bitch's milk than cow's milk, or you may decide to dispense with milk altogether. Many of the complete foods available for puppy rearing contain all the necessary nutrients, without any need for milk.

An erratic appetite can be a sign of worms, although they should not occur if the breeder has wormed the puppy correctly and if you have continued the worming routine (*see* Chapter 10). If you suspect that worms are the problem, consult your vet. You can buy worming products at pet shops, but the dosing instructions are often vague. An overdose can cause a severe stomach upset, and under-dosing will not stop the infestation.

If diarrhoea goes on for more than a day, and especially if the puppy seems listless, consult your vet immediately. A puppy with severe diarrhoea quickly becomes very ill.

Ch. Francehill Goodwill (rear) *and Ch. Francehill Florentine, owned and bred by Mrs Margaret Norman, née Searle.*

Vaccinations

Make appointments for vaccinations as soon as the new puppy arrives. Puppies are vaccinated against infectious canine hepatitis, leptospirosis, canine distemper and parvovirus, all of which are life-threatening conditions. There are normally two injections, the first at ten weeks, the second a fortnight later. The vet will advise you on the vaccination programme.

Socialization

A puppy should not be allowed to go for walks or to mix with other dogs until he has completed the course of injections. The early weeks are the most formative period of a puppy's life, however, and some owners try to make up for the enforced isolation, for instance by walking with the puppy in their arms so that he gets used to traffic and bustle.

Socialization is easier once a puppy is fully vaccinated. Time spent socializing your puppy is never wasted. It pays dividends, whether your dog is solely a pet, or a show dog coping with the crowds, noise and other dogs at competitions. A pet that shows obvious signs of distress when taken into strange environments is a pitiful sight, and show dogs have to be at ease in strange surroundings. It is increasingly difficult to take dogs to shops and public buildings, but it is important to try to find places where they can meet people. Some owners make a point of encouraging people to visit, others take the dog to collect children from school, an ideal way to introduce puppies (under careful supervision) to bustle in general and children in particular. Shelties that have not become accustomed to children as puppies rarely seem totally at ease with them as adults.

Lead-training

When a puppy has completed his course of vaccinations, he can go for short walks on a lead. This sounds simple enough, but a battle of wills often develops when the lead is first put on, with the puppy sitting and refusing to budge, or bucking and rearing with squeals of outrage. It helps to get the puppy used to wearing a collar for short periods indoors, then attaching a lead to the collar and allowing him to walk around dragging the lead behind him. Then try carrying him in your arms a few yards from your front gate before putting him down on the ground. With a little luck he will be so anxious to return to home territory that he will walk happily back with you holding the lead. The process of lead-training is often less stressful if you have older dogs that are going out on a lead – the puppy is so anxious not to be excluded from any fun that he forgets about the hindrance around his neck.

The first walks should be gentle meanders, as you allow the puppy to go where he chooses. Direction and control are more easily learned when your puppy is confident and relaxed, having associated the collar and lead with a pleasurable pastime.

It is extremely important to find a suitable collar and lead. Sheltie heads are narrow, and it is easy for a puppy that has been alarmed to

Ch. Felthorn Corn Flower, owned and bred by Mr and Mrs R. Thornley.
(*Photo. Diane Pearce.*)

Former breed-CC record-holders. Ch. Cultured at Cashella (rear),
bred by Mr and Mrs Macmillan and owned by Mr and Mrs Johnson,
and Ch. Mountmoor Blue Boy.

pull its head out of a conventional collar, unless the collar is fastened too tightly for comfort. We followed advice to use a rolled-leather collar on one of our earliest acquisitions. He was startled by traffic, retreated rapidly through his collar, and ran up the road, with me in hot pursuit. Since then we have always used a half-check collar: a nylon or leather strap with an adjustable buckle, attached to a short continuous chain onto which you clip the lead. The half-check collar is designed to tighten only as far as the buckle allows, which should be just tight enough not to pull over the head, and not so tight as to cause the dog any discomfort. The advantage of this collar is that it does not continue to tighten and choke the dog. A leather lead just under ½in (1cm) wide, is quite strong enough for a Sheltie. There is no need for Shelties to wear choke chains, which are far too heavy and can be dangerous.

Physical Development

Teething

A puppy's second set of teeth starts appearing at about four months. The gums surrounding the six top and six bottom incisors, at the front of the mouth, become red and swollen, before the new teeth break through. The milk teeth may fall out first, but do not panic if your puppy has a double row of teeth for a while, as the new teeth usually push the old ones out. Occasionally a tenacious milk tooth has to be removed. A puppy that is teething wants to chew hard things, and uses furniture, shoes and anything else he can find, if you do not provide an alternative. Hide chews and knuckle-bones are suitable. Bad chewing habits are extremely difficult to eradicate, so nip them in the bud. If he is chewing a chair leg, say 'No,' in a firm voice, and replace it with the bone or hide chew, praising him when he accepts.

The two upper and two lower canine teeth appear when a puppy reaches five months, and may cause more distress to the owner than to the dog himself. Misplaced canines are not common but do sometimes occur, and are counted as faults in the show ring. The upper canines should fit snugly behind, rather than in front of, the lower. If the canines appear to be growing into the correct position, even though the milk teeth are still in place, then there is no cause for concern. If you think that the retained baby teeth are impeding correct growth, or diverting the teeth, take the puppy to the vet to have the milk canines removed. Most vets extract the teeth with the aid of a whiff of gas. A general anaesthetic is not necessary, and fatalities occasionally occur when they are used.

The shedding of the molars at the back of the mouth may go on until the puppy is around ten months old. The teeth immediately behind the canines are called premolars, and new ones may fail to appear, or appear briefly and fall out, presumably because the roots are not big enough. The reason for this seems to be natural evolution. The domesticated dog does not need as many large teeth as his ancestors did to crush the bones of his prey, and dogs' teeth have gradually, over thousands of years, become much smaller. Even the skulls of dogs that died just one thousand years ago have larger teeth than modern dogs. Sheltie breeders in mainland Europe attach great importance to the tiny premolars, much more so than most British breeders, who feel that a missing tooth is insufficient grounds for disqualifying an otherwise excellent Sheltie.

Growth and Appearance

At around three-and-a-half months, the soft fluffy coat down the middle of a puppy's back starts to be replaced by straighter, probably darker, short hair. A puppy also begins to grow out of proportion, with his legs appearing far too long and his tail looking more like a piece of string. His head starts to lengthen and will quite possibly develop lumps and bumps in all the wrong places. Things get worse by the day before they get better, but get better they will.

It is more worrying when a puppy's ears either become erect, or droop like a spaniel's. These problems may be hereditary; but changes in ear carriage are also associated with teething, and seem to occur

The promise of things to come. Ch. Shelridge Ceilidh owned and bred by Mrs C. Aaron.

when the swollen gums press on the nerve that runs along the side of the mouth and up to the ear. You can usually make erect ears fall into the correct position by keeping the area where the ear should fall forward softened with hand lotion or glycerine. Treat more stubborn ears with a heavier greasing agent such as dubbin. Specialist equestrian shops sell a substance for repairing damaged hooves that works well and also encourages hair growth. Another remedy is a dab of kaolin mixed with talcum powder and stuck to the ear tip, the theory being that the weight on the tip will gradually wear off and leave the ear in a perfect position. Some owners claim total success with this method; others argue that putting weight on the ear tip will strengthen the ligaments and make the situation worse.

If the ears have become too heavy and are drooping, try removing a very little of the hair from the back of the ears, or, if you have a steady hand, from the inside of the ear tip. Be very careful: too much cutting may remove too much weight, which will cause the ears to become pricked. If trimming the hair does not work, you could try using a hessian splint to support the ear temporarily. Cut a piece of hessian to fit inside the ear up to the point where it should fall forward, and secure the splint with a non-irritant adhesive such as gum arabic, available from most chemist's shops.

Correct ear carriage can be inherited, and these problems are far less likely to occur if you have chosen your puppy from a breeder who has concentrated on this quality. Some quite elaborate devices for correcting ears are in use, especially in America, but many breeders would think they had failed if their puppies needed them.

Six Months

At six months a Sheltie should have all his teeth in the right places (although he may still shed molars), and enough coat to give an idea of the luxuriant growth to come. He will have regained the correct body proportions, and his head and expression are infinitely more pleasing, although his foreface may still look a little angular, and his rump may still appear a little higher than his withers. His ears may have become erect or too heavy when he started teething but now fall correctly most of the time. He also has two testicles fully descended into the scrotum. Your well-reared, fully house-trained and lead-trained, well-adjusted puppy is almost ready to assume his role as a loyal companion, or to start the long quest for honours in the show ring.

5

Adolescent and Adult Management

The appearance of the Shetland Sheepdog has changed radically since the early 1900s, but the modern dog has retained the hardiness, desire to please, unswerving loyalty, and great intelligence of his ancestors. He has also inherited the capacity to form intense ties of mutual affection with his owners, just as his ancestors developed a bond with the island crofters and shepherds whose lives often depended on their willing dogs. Owners no longer depend on the Sheltie in that way, but he is still happiest in an environment that encourages him to display this highly developed characteristic.

This is not to say that Shelties should be kept only singly, although they seem perfectly happy when they are. Their forefathers usually lived several together in crofts, and modern Shelties accept and enjoy the company of other dogs. The cost of food, insurance and vet's bills must be considered, however, and the ideal number of dogs for any owner depends on circumstances. Common sense dictates that the quality of life, for owners and dogs, decreases when too many dogs are kept.

Shelties are lovable, relatively easy to look after, and live well into their teens. These are desirable qualities, but the effect of them is that many breeders who originally intend to have only a few dogs actually find themselves keeping a large pack. A puppy kept from the first litter is joined by a more promising one from the second, the third, and so on, until a sea of Shelties greets them in the morning. There may be local regulations that affect the number of dogs you can have, so check thoroughly with the relevant local authority before committing yourself to a course that you may have to change, with distressing consequences, in the future.

Some of the regulations affecting dogs are understandable, particularly those intended to enforce hygiene and prevent noise. It is possible that a lone Sheltie kept as a pet can be trained to curtail his natural tendency to bark loudly at every passer-by, but a pack of Shelties is virtually impossible to silence. In America, Shelties (and other breeds) sometimes have their vocal cords cut to solve the problem – a surgical procedure called 'debarking'. I found the husky, coughing noise produced by the debarked Sheltie rather distressing, although the dogs seem to enjoy the process of barking just as much.

Exercising a large number of dogs may also present problems. Two or three Shelties can exercise freely in suitable open spaces, but more are much harder to control. Excitement is highly contagious, and renders the most obedient dog temporarily deaf. The sight of a pack of shrieking Shelties rushing towards an unwary, totally innocent intruder on their favourite exercise area is not at all pleasant, and understandably tends to sour relationships with neighbours.

Edglonian Rather Prity, owned and bred by Mr J. R. Pearson.

Diet

From six or seven months of age, a Sheltie needs only one main meal per day. This is the most natural routine for a modern dog, because he still has the same slow-working digestive system as his hunting ancestors. He should be fed at about the same time each day, but it does not matter when this is. Most owners give a biscuit or two in the morning if the main meal is fed in the evening, and vice versa. Dogs should have access to fresh water at all times, and there should be plenty of it if they eat a complete food.

How much food to give depends on the Sheltie. Dogs have different metabolisms and different levels of activity, just as people do. A lively dog that has plenty of exercise will need significantly more than one that only potters about in the garden. Complete foods come with charts showing recommended quantities for dogs of different weights, but these tend to be on the generous side for most adult Shelties. Finding out what is right for your dog is a matter of trial and error, combined with careful monitoring of the dog's weight, health and fitness.

Complete foods have many advantages. They save time and work, and they take the guesswork out of providing the correct balance of nutrients. Dogs that eat complete foods also produce stools of a good consistency, a significant advantage in a long-coated breed. Some of the qualities that the manufacturers promise are not so desirable for this breed, however – for example earlier maturity, heavier bone and more coat. Shelties are notoriously late maturing, the Breed Standard says they should not look coarse or cloddy, and too much coat significantly alters the outline and balance.

Some owners prefer to give a more traditional diet of fresh or tinned meat, with biscuit meal. Half a pound of meat and biscuit meal is generally sufficient for an adult Sheltie, although the pregnant or nursing bitch will need considerably more. An elderly Sheltie needs less protein, so the proportion of meat in his diet should be reduced. Too much meat may cause his kidneys to fail as they try to break down the unused protein. The biscuit provides essential carbohydrates, which can also be provided as flaked cereal, soaked in stock or hot water, and mixed with the meat to a muesli-like consistency. Too much carbohydrate makes a dog fat but too little leads to stomach upsets, as does too much fat in the meat.

Adult dogs do not need milk. Some enjoy it, but it tends to cause loose motions. Egg yolks can be given quite safely, but egg whites

Ch. Rannerdale Golden Shot, Ch. Rannerdale Bertie Wooster and Rannerdale Miss Pebbles.

contain an element that destroys vitamins, and should never be given. Chewing bones from time to time is good for the jaws and teeth of both adult dogs and puppies. Give only large marrow bones – other bones (not only chicken bones), can splinter and cause serious injuries.

Occasionally, a dog frets and loses weight if he is aware of a bitch in season, and some virtually stop eating for the duration. This is a temporary problem, but it is worrying for the owner of a stud-dog or show dog. The dog refuses even the most tempting morsels, and even the competition of a feeding mate fails to stir his appetite. Some owners find a homoeopathic remedy useful at these times.

Housing

A Sheltie who lives in the home should have his own bed. It can be a cardboard box, or a purpose-made item such as a wicker basket, bean bag or foam-filled bed. It does not have to be very big: Shelties seem to like curling themselves up into small corners. Whatever the sort of bed, you should be able to shake out the bedding and wash it. Like any dog, a Sheltie enjoys lounging in a comfortable armchair if he can. Whether or not you allow this does not really matter, as long as you are consistent about it. Some owners give a dog his own chair, as a compromise.

Kennels

Shelties are happiest in the home, but they can adapt to kennel life as long as they have companionship. A Sheltie kept in solitary confinement

Int. Ch. Ingleside Copper Image, a dominant sire, imported to Sweden by Begrime and Per Svarstaad.

soon becomes morose and withdrawn. Shelties kennelled in pairs or in larger communities usually live together peacefully, the envy of breeders of more quarrelsome types of dog. If you intend the kennels to be a business you must consider the national legislation on keeping dogs, and local authority regulations for your own area. You should in any case find out if planning permission is required for any kennel structure. You should also ask the local authority first if you want to use an incinerator for waste.

Kennels vary from small units capable of housing two Shelties together, to large structures containing enclosures like loose boxes for individual dogs. These give the dogs more room if they have to be kept in for any reason. Whatever the type of kennel, the dogs should have snug individual boxes, or benches raised at least 12in (30cm) from the floor, with a raised lip on the outside edge to help retain bedding. The kennel must be free of draughts in cold weather and cool in hot weather. Fit wire-panelled inner doors to allow the air to move freely on hot days, and have shutters on all the windows to preserve heat in the winter months. The size, type and number of windows is important, as heat escapes through them in cold weather, and on warmer days the hot sun pouring in through them can quickly transform a small room into an oven.

Good hygiene is essential. Remove faeces frequently and dispose of them in an incinerator or sunken waste disposal unit, having checked your waste disposal plans with the local authority before installing any sort of unit if several dogs are involved. Daily power-washing and disinfecting of runs should be standard practice, as should the washing and disinfecting of sleeping quarters. Use bedding that can be disposed of or kept clean. Blankets and other types of fabric bedding should be washed regularly. Shredded paper and wood wool can be renewed daily, and any soiled bedding disposed of immediately. Sawdust should be treated in the same way, although it is not an ideal bedding material because the small particles can cause eye irritation. Wood shavings are sometimes recommended, but you have to be very sure that the wood has not been treated. We almost lost Ch. Hartmere Harris Tweed at twelve weeks through poisoning from shavings of wood that had been treated despite assurances to the contrary from the supplier.

A kennel should not need heating in winter as long as the dogs have warm, draught-free beds. The one exception is that a heat source is essential even in summer for bitches that whelp in a kennel. All electrical installations should be carried out by a qualified craftsman, who should ensure that wires are securely protected from Sheltie teeth.

The positioning of your kennel needs careful thought. If access is very easy and convenient for you, it may be equally so for unwanted visitors. A kennel too near a boundary fence may cause friction with the neighbours. Shelties have a reputation for being incessant barkers. This is not really fair, but it has to be said that they voice their protests if they see or hear people or animals they do not know well, so do not place your kennel where dogs can see passers-by or neighbours innocently working in their gardens.

Kennel Runs

Frequent free exercise is essential for dogs kept in kennels. Some kennels include a small yard, which is adequate for toilet needs, but dogs need much more space to maintain good physical and mental health. Ideally dogs should be able to roam freely in a large garden with a securely fenced boundary. Shelties are very inquisitive, and soon organize escape committees if left to their own devices. If dogs cannot have the run of the garden, build the largest kennel runs that space allows, so that the dogs can play. They should be able to run at least a few strides before encountering a fence, and you must take them out for regular exercise.

If you can afford to, roof the runs with tinted, ridged reinforced plastic sheets to make them useful in all weathers. This is expensive, but is much better for the dogs than keeping them shut in their kennels when you think they might expose themselves to too much rain or sun outside. A roofed run must be very well sited and constructed to withstand gales. Trees give some protection from extremes of weather, but are only partly effective. Rigid tinted panels are also useful when secured vertically to fencing, as they give shade when the sun is not directly overhead, and shelter from rain carried on the wind.

Fencing should be 6ft (2m)-high weld-mesh panels, or correctly tightened chain links on posts concreted firmly into the ground. Shelties are adept at finding ways to escape from kennels and runs. Sink the fencing into the ground, and fit stout weld mesh gates, preferably double gates so the outer gate can be securely fastened before the inner gate is opened.

Grass or gravel runs are aesthetically pleasing, but are a major headache to keep clean and free of germs. Dogs kept wholly on grass may develop splayed feet, and their nails need constant attention because they never wear down on the soft surface. Grass is also a high-maintenance surface. It needs regular mowing so that grass seeds do not

Ch. Tegwell Sandwick Storm, owned by Ray Grice and bred by Mrs J. Stanley. (Photo. Jackson.)

form and get into eyes or between pads, and dogs quickly churn the best-kept lawn into mud during rainy spells. Concrete or stone-paved runs are less attractive to look at, but infinitely more practical. They are easy to keep clean and disinfected, and the hard abrasive surface helps to keep nails short and feet tight. Slate slabs have the advantage of drying quickly, but can become very slippery during frosty weather. To help drainage, lay the runs so that they slope down slightly from the kennels. Dig a soak-away and partly fill the bottom with stones.

Keep the runs clean and clear, but be very careful when using chemicals to do so. Always follow the manufacturers' instructions precisely when using bleach or disinfectant, and use garden pesticides and weedkillers with extreme caution. A supposedly safe weedkiller blinded and paralysed one of our dogs: luckily he responded to immediate treatment, but we might have lost him. Controlling vermin with toxic substances is not an option for a dog-owner.

If you want a Sheltie to exercise freely in the garden, make sure that any toxic plants are inaccessible. A good gardening encyclopaedia will tell you which plants might cause upsets or worse. Many Shelties are themselves enthusiastic amateur gardeners, and any treasured borders should be securely fenced.

Exercise

However well housed a Sheltie is, and however spacious his run or garden, he will always benefit from a daily walk. A Sheltie needs mental stimulation as well as physical exertion for his health and well-being, and walking provides both. It is a wonderful way to cement the relationship between dog and owner, and helps the owner to understand the dog better. A Sheltie has an excellent coat, and can go out even in heavy rain, providing he is thoroughly towelled dry afterwards.

Exercise has to be structured to be effective. A slow amble will be of little benefit and, if you intend to show your dog, will merely ensure that you add to the swollen ranks of short-stepping dogs in the ring. The daily walk should include plenty of free running (obviously easier with two or more dogs) to build and tone muscle, and to expand and deepen the rib cage. Twisting and turning, exploring hedgerows and bushes, and jumping over rocks and fallen trees are great fun and physically and mentally stimulating, but they are also essential for developing the agility and lithe movement that are principal requirements for the breed. Roadwork tightens and strengthens ligaments and sinews and wears down nails. If you maintain the correct speed it also lengthens your dog's stride, provided he is correctly constructed. As part of their daily walk, our dogs are taken along an old country lane with a natural surface of small stones, which tightens their feet. I learned this from the breeders of racing Whippets, whose dogs I used to exercise for the princely reward of one shilling (5p) when I was in my early teens.

Finding suitable areas where dogs can run free is becoming more and more difficult, but it is essential for your Sheltie to be able to run over undulating and rough ground if you wish him to look and move at his best in the show ring. When I judge, I am often dismayed at the poor thigh-muscle tone of exhibits, and am never surprised to see such dogs move with virtually no drive and propulsion from behind.

Grooming

Preparation for the show ring is covered in Chapter 7. Basic grooming is largely a matter of common sense, and should be an enjoyable part of owning a Sheltie, whose luxuriant coat is such an appealing feature. If grooming is neglected, or if a Sheltie does not become accustomed to it from an early age, it can develop into an unpleasant battle of wills.

Brushing

When they are about six weeks old, puppies can be taught to stand on a worktop on which a rubber-backed mat has been placed for stability. Although there is hardly enough coat to groom at this age, they become accustomed to the ritual. This is a good habit for breeders to adopt, as the puppies that leave for other homes think of grooming as a pleasurable experience. Use a soft hair brush, the sort designed for babies, to brush the coat lightly along the back. Gradually extend the brushing to the chest and rear end, and, eventually, gently persuade the puppy gently to lie down so that each side can be brushed in turn. Once accustomed to this, a Sheltie relaxes completely, which makes thorough grooming much easier when he grows his heavy adult coat.

Owners with only one or two dogs may even become over-diligent with grooming. Too vigorous and frequent brushing with the wrong brush can remove healthy hair. To maximize a Sheltie's glamour, and to keep him looking presentable, groom little and often, with one very thorough session a week.

A brush with bristles and long nylon tines set in a rubber cushion allows thorough grooming down to the skin, removing dead hair and stimulating hair growth. High-street shops sell brushes like this for human use. It is much easier to groom a coat that has been dampened. Use rainwater, and add just a few drops of any pleasant-smelling spirit-based substance, such as after-shave or perfume. The spirit helps to control excess grease that could trap dust and give rise to unpleasant odours and skin disorders. Be sparing: too much spirit removes the dog's natural oils, leaving the coat dry, with a frizzy, unnatural look and texture. It also ruins the rubber cushion on the brush, causing the bristles to fall out.

The most effective way to dampen the coat is with a small plastic spray bottle, of the type used to mist indoor plants. When the coat is thoroughly damp, start to brush along the back, towards the head, holding the coat in one hand and brushing small segments from underneath

Ch. Morestyle Monsoon, a multiple CC winner, owned and bred by Mrs E. Wilson. (Photo. Jackson.)

the hand as you go. Lay the Sheltie on his side to brush the coat upwards over the ribs towards the spine, and then brush back the other way. Turn your dog gently onto the other side and repeat the procedure.

Pay particular attention to the tail and breeching where the coat is longest, and do not forget to thoroughly brush the insides of the thighs and armpits, where the finer, silkier hair can soon become matted if neglected. Gently tease out small mats in these areas with fingers and comb. Large mats are best cut out. If the coat becomes dry before you have finished grooming, spray again, as brushing can break dry hair. Stand the dog up and brush the hair back into place, with long sweeping strokes towards the tail, and then comb the hair behind his ears and on the back of his front legs with a steel comb. Finish by gently pulling a wide-toothed steel comb through the coat, starting at the head and carrying the stroke on towards the tail.

A Sheltie's coat does not need extensive trimming to keep it looking tidy, but any long, unsightly hair inside the ears can be shortened with scissors. The finer trimming of ears, feet and hocks is outlined in Chapter 7.

Feet and Nails

Check your Shelties feet weekly, and cut off any long hair growing between the pads. This will prevent mud and small stones becoming lodged there, which can cause lameness. At the same time, check that the nails are not too long, and if necessary shorten them very carefully. Use a guillotine nail clipper to slice through the nail, rather than conventional clippers, as the latter have a crushing action. Many owners are apprehensive about clipping nails, but no discomfort or bleeding will occur if the cut is made below the quick. It is easy to see the quick as a dark area in white nails. If a dog has black nails, a faint grey line around the nail shows the end of the living portion. A cut below this line is completely safe. Accidents can happen though, and you should always have a small tub of potassium permanganate handy to stop any bleeding immediately.

Bathing

Some owners say that a well-groomed Sheltie never needs bathing; others advise that dry cleaning with powder is all that is required. Powdering may seem simple, but brushing all the powder out is actually very hard work. Any residue may provoke skin irritation, and powdering a dirty, greasy coat makes it tacky and messy.

There is nothing quite like the sheen produced by a bath. A Sheltie should be bathed whenever he needs to be, and at least once a month to keep his coat in good condition. When he is losing his coat, a bath after a thorough grooming shortens the period of hair loss. A bath may also be necessary if he rolls in obnoxious substances, a pastime that dogs find deeply satisfying, but their owners find repulsive. It is an instinctive habit that dogs have inherited from their wild ancestors who, it is thought, indulged in the behaviour as a means of concealing their natural scent when stalking their quarry. Whether or not your dog regularly displays this tendency, a Sheltie is simply more pleasant to be with if he is bathed regularly.

Shelties are resigned and fatalistic at bath times, rather than obstructive and defiant. You can do very little to make the process enjoyable, but you can considerably reduce the time the dog feels sorry for himself if you organize everything in advance. A thorough groom before the bath helps enormously, removing dead hair and separating the coat to allow quicker soaking by the water.

Some owners bathe their dogs in a sink at waist height, others use the family bath. A showerhead on a flexible pipe helps to soak the coat completely before the shampoo is applied. The mildest human shampoo is perfectly adequate, but a vet can provide a special solution for a dog that has fleas or other parasites.

Massage the shampoo into the coat thoroughly, avoiding the head and ears, but including legs and feet, then rinse well. Repeat the procedure until you have a good lather, and give a final rinse. Bathing makes the coat feel softer, so use a good-quality conditioner to restore the natural texture a little quicker. Conditioner made for humans will do. Rinse the coat again, then squeeze the water from the back, and down the legs and feet, before wrapping the dog in a large bath towel.

The long Sheltie hair can be split and broken by vigorous towelling, so allow the water to be absorbed into the towel while you carry your dog to a suitable place for him to shake himself vigorously. He will shake out water droplets no matter how long he has been in the towel, so be careful where you put him.

A Sheltie can be brushed dry if he is bathed on a warm summer's day, but on cool days use a hair-dryer set on low heat to dry the coat quickly and easily. Brush in the way described earlier. Introduce a puppy to a hair-dryer gradually, and he will learn to accept and even enjoy the warm air blowing through his coat. Remember that the belly and inner thigh are not as well covered with coat as other parts of the body, so keep the air stream moving to avoid any discomfort. Never direct warm air onto the head.

Vaccination Boosters

The usual advice is to give dogs booster injections every year to upgrade their immunity levels, but concerns have been raised about side-effects, and given breeders cause for serious thought. The fact that humans are inoculated at far less frequent intervals has also prompted much questioning of the current veterinary advice. We have carried out blood tests on our adult dogs, and found that their levels of antibodies are considerably higher than they need to be to fight off infection, which suggests there is no need to increase their immunity levels further. There is also evidence that the four principal viruses covered by the inoculation programme no longer constitute a threat in Britain,

Ch. Milesend Storm Warden (aged fourteen months), a multiple CC winner owned and bred by Mrs J. Miles.

and that any future outbreaks are likely to be mutations of the original viruses. Inoculation is unlikely to provide any protection against these. Some breeders who are anxious that inoculation may cause serious side effects, while not providing the protection needed, have turned to homoeopathic nosodes. These are thought to increase the dog's ability to repel viruses, but do not have side-effects.

Old Age

Shelties are a relatively slow-maturing breed. A Sheltie still looks and behaves like a young dog at an age when many other breeds are beginning to show signs of ageing. When a Sheltie does begin to slow down a little, his protein requirement diminishes significantly, as discussed under Diet, above. Feed elderly dogs two small meals a day instead of

119

one large one. Each meal should be about 12 per cent easily digestible protein.

Older Shelties enjoy extra treats, and seem to enjoy their senior status. Shelties that in their youth were anything but lap dogs, become them in later life. Their characters develop, and they take advantage of their owners, secure in the knowledge that allowances are always made for age. Elderly Shelties are generally infrequent visitors to the vet's surgery, and they remain quite fit and able into ripe old age. The first sign of ageing is usually a slight hearing loss. This does not seem to bother the dog, although it may be a nuisance for the owner. Progressive retinal atrophy (PRA), a disease of the eye that leads inevitably to blindness, occurs far less frequently than was once thought (see Chapter 8). Older Shelties may be slightly stiff after lying down for long periods, and extra oil in their diet can be beneficial. Arthritis or may be the cause (see Chapter 10).

The older Sheltie becomes an endearing and important part of the owner's life. The dog's old age is a special but finite time for both. Unfortunately very few Shelties pass away peacefully in their sleep. They cling on to life with surprising and often distressing tenacity, and this makes the decision to end their suffering all the harder. Reluctance to accept a final parting is natural, but when the time comes – and you will usually be able to judge this from the difficult to define but unmistakable look in his eyes – try not to flinch from this last act of kindness. Euthanasia, which is performed by the vet using a large dose of sedative, is a quick and painless way to end a dog's suffering. If you are nervous about what it entails, ask your vet to explain the procedure to you. Then, when the moment arrives – and hard though it is to appear normal and calm – you owe it to your companion to make his passing as stress-free as possible, which means staying with him to reassure him. To deny him your support by abandoning him in these last moments is a mean betrayal of his trust.

Another Dog?

Grief at losing a companion is natural and understandable, and the immediate reaction is to decide not to become close to another dog. Owners also feel guilty at the thought that a new dog might steal their affection. However, you could think of it as a fitting tribute to your old friend to open a new chapter. Another dog never replaces the old one exactly, but eases the feeling of loss and brings new joy and companionship.

6

Showing

Showing dogs is expensive, time consuming and often disheartening. It can also become a passion. The urge to show animals in competition seems to go very deep. As long ago as the 13th century, there were competitions for the best hounds reared by tenants as part of their feudal duties. Modern owners routinely spend days preparing their dogs, and then get up before dawn to drive to a venue lacking in all but the most basic amenities. They show their dogs, and may win a card or, if they are very lucky, a rosette, but are more likely to go away empty-handed and to arrive home late, with just enough time to feed their dogs (and perhaps themselves) before collapsing into bed with exhaustion. Those who are already involved in this bizarre way of life will recognize this description. But – as those who have yet to enter into it will discover – the rewards are many, not least of which are the friendship of fellow exhibitors, and the chance to pool knowledge and contribute to the improvement of the breed.

Types of Show

There are four main types of show available in the UK: exemption shows, primary shows, open shows and, finally, championship shows (at which Challenge Certificates are on offer).

Exemption Shows

These are the least formal shows, and are often held as part of a fete or other fundraising event. They are licensed by the Kennel Club, but are exempt from some of its rules, hence the name. Pedigree dogs (not necessarily registered with the Kennel Club), and non-pedigree dogs can take part. Only five classes for pedigree dogs are allowed, but there can be any number of novelty classes, such as 'Dog with the Waggiest Tail', or 'Dog in Best Condition'. Entries are on arrival.

121

Ch. Willow Tarn True Love, owned and bred by Mrs R. Crossley.

Primary Shows

Entry is open only to members of the organizing club or society, and entries are taken on arrival. No more than eight classes may be scheduled, and the highest class is maiden (for dogs that have not previously won an adult class). These are shows for inexperienced dogs, and are useful for beginner exhibitors.

Open Shows

Open shows are open to all dogs including champions and CC winners. There may be classes for Any Variety in addition to classes for specific breeds. There are usually four classes for each breed: puppy, junior, post-graduate and open

Championship Shows

These shows are open to all dogs (with the exception of Crufts, for which dogs qualify by wins or placings in specified classes at the other championship shows). The Kennel Club awards CCs (Challenge Certificates) to the dog and bitch judged best in each breed. Wins and places in specific classes qualify for entry in the Stud Book. Stakes classes, for puppies, veterans and champions of all breeds, are a feature of general championship shows, and unlike the breed classes, often have prize money donated by the commercial sponsors of the classes.

Entering Shows

The dog press carries advertisements for shows, giving the address of the show secretary. For any that you wish to enter you must send a stamped addressed envelope for a show schedule. You will automatically be sent a schedule and entry form for all the shows of a breed club or general canine society of which you are a member.

The schedule contains an entry form and all the information you need, including the date, time and place of the show, and the names of judges. Note the times of classes carefully. Arriving too late to be judged is a soul-destroying experience. Breeds are listed alphabetically, and the different classes are described and numbered. A full definition of the classes is given at the back of the schedule, so that you can check that you are entering your dog in a class for which he is eligible. A dog cannot win an award in a class for which he is ineligible.

The entry form has columns for the dog's name, date of birth, and breeding details, and for the classes you wish to enter. Entry forms must be returned before the closing date given.

Show Training

Breeders start gentle show training when puppies are still very young. A promising puppy can be standing on the grooming table by the time he is six weeks old, while the owner goes through the motions of assessing, or 'going over', him as a judge would. This means raising his ears to the desired position to assess his expression, and running the hands over his topline and down his shoulder and upper arm, to check for correct angulation.

This early introduction to standing on a table for examination is an ideal way to start preparing the potential show dog. If he thinks of it as an extension of the time spent playing with his owner, he stands on the table without any trepidation when he attends his first show. It is helpful if friends and fellow breeders also look at a puppy on the table (if you are sure that they will handle him gently), so he becomes familiar with the touch of others.

A dog must also learn to stand in show pose and to walk by your side on a lead for the judge to assess his movement. The best way for dog and handler to learn show skills is by attending the ring-training classes run by breed clubs and local canine societies. Experienced exhibitors act out the part of judge at these classes, and give help and advice to the novice. Many experienced exhibitors use the classes to train young dogs, and to accustom them to meeting other people and dogs in a show situation. You may find classes just for Shelties, or for all breeds. It is useful for a dog to meet other breeds, but you might like to watch a mixed class before taking your dog along. Any large and aggressive dogs that are under less than expert control are apt to disrupt the proceedings, and could undermine a Sheltie's confidence.

Whether or not training classes are held in your area, visit shows that schedule Shelties. Watch how the handlers move their dogs for the judge, and attract their dogs' attention when the judge is looking. Most handlers give help and advice if asked politely after judging is completed, but do not expect to become expert overnight. Your own skill needs time to develop, and every dog requires different handling to bring out his best in the ring. Good handling means promoting a dog in an easy, unobtrusive manner. A handler does not have to be a performer, and self-conscious novice handlers should remember that it is the dog that is being judged, not the handler.

Traditionally Shelties are shown free standing, on a lead. Training in standing properly can start very young. A Sheltie puppy is extremely inquisitive, and watches your every movement with a frank, alert enthusiasm. Use this behaviour to train him to stand and show to his best advantage in the ring, by concealing and revealing an object in your hand. The puppy treats this as a game, and with a little practice and encouragement learns to stand and watch your hand while in show pose.

Many exhibitors keep a tasty treat concealed in the hand, but other objects may be produced to encourage a reluctant shower. One successful breeder always wore an apron while handling her dogs, and produced all sorts of objects from the pocket, including on one

124

Mrs Lyn French demonstrates perfect handling technique with her
Ch. Hartmere Hayday at Lirren, bred by Patti and Malcolm Hart.

occasion a chicken wing complete with feathers. An edible treat is not necessarily the best thing to hold. It attracts the dog's attention, and he certainly stands alert, ears perfectly placed to capture the faintest sound of rustling, but greed may transform those lovely, almond-shaped, medium-sized eyes into large round orbs that are quite wrong. The practice of double handling, in which a second handler attracts the attention of the dog, is banned by most Kennel Clubs, and the penalties for it are severe.

Shelties have a natural aptitude for walking in the ring. Usually, the judge asks a handler to move in a triangle, in order to see the dog's action as he moves away, then sideways on, and as he comes back. This manoeuvre is always carried out with the dog on the handler's left, but do train your dog to walk on your right, as you may be asked to walk back across the ring while the judge assesses the profile movement, and you must not walk between the judge and your dog. Dogs that have been taught to walk only on the left become totally confused when directed to the right, and refuse to walk correctly.

Show training should be fun for both you and your Sheltie. A puppy should learn to accept training as a natural, everyday occurrence. Lessons should always be short, and should be rewarded with an extended, informal play time. Dogs of any age, and puppies especially, are not machines, and dogs that are relaxed and happy to show look better in the ring than highly disciplined exhibits standing like statues.

Am. & Can. Ch. Kensil's Kings Lady, bred and owned by David and Sylvia Calderwood. (Photo. Dan Burkhart.)

Care of the Show Dog

Ring-training and skilful handling are essential, but they are not enough to ensure success in the ring. Good show presentation begins long before you arrive in the ring, and even before you place your dog on a grooming table. Newcomers to the breed may feel that a Sheltie's natural beauty can hardly be improved upon, and up to a point this is correct – if the basics aren't there, nothing can create them. But there is much that can be done to draw out the best that nature has given your dog.

A correct diet is the first essential element of show presentation. A dog needs plenty of tissue-building proteins to develop the muscle tone reflected in both movement and stance, and to grow a long, full and luxuriant coat. There is no easy formula for the percentage of protein to feed, and you may find that food manufacturers give contradictory information. Use common sense and careful observation of your dog. A diet that is too rich is potentially as harmful as one that is too poor.

Fats and oils also contribute to healthy coat growth, and some complete foods for growing dogs contain just the right amount to help maintain your dog in show condition. They are also high in protein. If you feed your dog on a more traditional diet, add a teaspoonful of sunflower oil, or a knob of butter. You might also increase his meat allowance slightly.

The protein and calories in this enhanced diet supply the extra energy required for exercise, which is the second vital element in show presentation. A dog must have the right amount of toned muscle in order to move correctly. In our eagerness to produce technically correct Shelties, with all their bones and joints set at the correct angles, it is perhaps too easy sometimes to forget the importance of good diet and appropriate exercise, both of which are simple matters that can improve your dog immeasurably.

Owners are sometimes anxious that too much exercise will produce too much muscle. They may have read that galloping up hills develops too much muscle in the hindquarters, leading to wide rear movement, or that galloping down hills puts the shoulders too wide apart. In this writer's opinion, such warnings should be ignored. A well-constructed, well-proportioned adult Sheltie should be able to negotiate the roughest terrain, and the physical and mental stimulation of free exercise over broken, stony ground, and among bushes and trees, is completely beneficial.

Show Grooming

A Sheltie's coat must be completely clean for grooming to produce the best results. Bathe a dog all over, after first brushing him through, five days before the show, and use a hair-dryer to dry his coat. Bathing makes even the harshest coat softer than it should be, but five days is ample time for it to recover. Thoroughly groom the dog in four directions every day thereafter, and bathe the white markings again on the evening before the show. Bathing and grooming methods are described in Chapter 5. The rainwater-based coat spray described there is suitable for show grooming as well.

Various types of coat spray can be bought, but these may leave a slightly tacky residue on the coat and produce the wrong coat texture. Under Kennel Club rules, when a dog is exhibited no substance can be left in its coat which is designed to change its colour or texture. Random checks are carried out at major shows, and transgressors can be and have been banned from exhibiting. It is also against Kennel Club rules to use chalk, so do not clean your dog with chalk at the show, and do ensure that no chalk remains in the coat if you have used any in your preparations at home.

The normal grooming regime should include keeping a dog's ears, feet and hocks trimmed, and his teeth clean. The final trimming for a show should be carried out no later than the bath day, five days before. Shelties do not require much special trimming for the show ring. The dog should look neat, but any tidying up should be subtle. An artificial, sculptured look would be quite wrong.

Start with the ears. Some Shelties seem to have far more hair here than others, and it is impossible to say how much should be taken off. You should remove just enough to avoid an unkempt, straggly appearance, in the way described below, but keep enough to give a soft, natural look. Most owners learn through careful observation of the breed, and some trial and error. It also helps to use the carpenter's maxim – think twice, cut once.

A heavily coated dog often has very thick and long hair at the back of his ears, and long, silky, paler hair growing from the base. The traditional way to thin it while keeping the ears looking natural, was to pluck it out with thumb and finger, often with the help of chalk to improve the grip. An expert can produce a perfect look with this method, but not without causing the dog some discomfort. Thinning scissors, with one blade serrated and the other straight, give the same effect without the discomfort. Always cut in the direction of the hair, and never cut against it. Pause frequently to comb the thinned hair, until it blends naturally into the surrounding coat.

Next, use thinning scissors to remove any long straggly hair growing from the inside of the ear, both from the base and upwards on the inside edge. The outside edge should now be easy to see. Trim the pale, uneven hair that grows from the base to roughly where the ear tips forward. Trimming scissors give a blurred, soft edge to the hair, whereas straight-bladed scissors give an unnaturally straight cut edge. If your dog has heavy ears, tidy the ear tips with thinning scissors, following the line of the ear tip. If your dog has high ear carriage, do not be tempted to remove any hair, or you may end up with a prick-eared Sheltie.

The feet should be neat and oval in shape. Trim round the outside of each front foot using straight-edged scissors. It is important to get this

Int. Ch. Nigma Saffron, Australian import to Sweden, bred by Barbara and Jeff Phillips, owned by Birgita and Per Svarstaad.

Sheer enjoyment. Agility champion Starbelle Satin Slippers, bred by Madeleine Lund.

right. If you cut the hair covering the nail too short, the foot will look round. If you leave it too long, the dog will have an ugly and incorrect 'hare foot'. Shorten the hair between the pads underneath the feet, then stand back and assess the results. If any unsightly tufts are sticking up between the toes, pull them down between the toes and shorten them from beneath, taking care not to remove so much that the toes appear separated and splayed.

Comb the hair on the back of the pasterns out and away from the leg, and check its length. If it is long and straggly, shorten it a little with the thinning scissors. Avoid cutting this hair in a straight line. It makes it

130

look too barbered, and if the cut is sloping, an optical illusion gives the pasterns a weak look. A straight vertical cut makes the pasterns appear too upright.

Treat the hind feet in the same way as the front feet, and comb the long thick hair on the back of the hocks away from the leg. Some owners shorten this hair with long-bladed, straight-edged scissors, but this gives a rather artificial look. The steady-handed can soften the appearance with a duplex trimmer (a razorblade clamped between two metal plates with serrated edges). It is easiest to use serrated scissors, starting at the point of the hock and cutting towards the foot. Take care not to remove too much hair, or you will produce an unnatural, knobbly effect. Use thinning scissors to give a more contoured and natural look, by taking another cut at the inside and outside edges of the initial cut. Finish off by shortening any hair that remains as a fringe around the large pad. The hock should now look natural and tidy, with just enough hair removed to give the correct thickness of leg. There is a growing tendency for exhibitors to leave copious quantities of hair on the hock, and then brush it out straight, making the legs look twice as thick as they really are!

American exhibitors tend to trim other parts of the coat, to enhance or disguise certain features. In particular the head may be trimmed to disguise a skull that is too rounded, too broad, or too deep. It is very hard to do this successfully, because the scissor marks always show. The colour of each hair varies along its length, and cutting alters the smoothly blended, natural patterning, producing solid, unnatural blocks of colour.

Bathe the dog's white markings on the eve of the show.

Final Preparations

Pack your show bag the night before the show, but check well beforehand that you have all the things you need.

Combs and brushes Keep these in a smaller bag with several pockets for easy access. A hairdresser's equipment bag is ideal, and folds up to fit snugly into the show bag.

Coat spray Check that it does not infringe Kennel Club regulations.

Baby wipes For cleaning stains from white legs and feet.

Show leads Always take a spare.

Ring number clip For holding the number that the steward gives you.

Benching chain To fasten your dog if the show is benched and you do not want him confined to a cage.

Benching towel

Show bait The treats or other items that you use to encourage your dog to show well in the ring

Make sure that you know exactly where the show is being held and how to get there, before going to bed. In the morning, set off early. Allow time for the dog to settle into his surroundings, and for the final grooming before you enter the ring.

If your preparation for the show has been thorough, you should need only to spray the dog's coat and brush him thoroughly from tail to head until dry. This will raise and separate the hairs. These are finishing touches only: brush lightly rather than attacking the coat. Brush the coat back into place, comb the hair behind the ears and front legs, and finish off by drawing a wide-toothed comb smoothly through the coat. Finally comb the hair on the back of the hocks towards the ground, slip on a clean show lead and take your dog to the ring.

In the Ring

Prior to your debut as an exhibitor, you may have attended many shows as a spectator and observed the experienced handlers as, with no apparent effort, they display their charges to the maximum effect. You will have practised your own ringcraft skills, and your young hopeful will have been schooled to move and show off his virtues to an imaginary judge in the privacy of your garden. Quite correctly, you will be brimming with confidence in your ability. If only that were all that is needed to ensure that your first showing experience will be both enjoyable and memorable, for the right reasons!

There are mercifully few official rules and regulations governing conduct in the ring, and most are a combination of plain common sense and good manners. The Kennel Club can impose fines and/or suspension on exhibitors who are proved to have behaved discreditably. But few incidents are ever deemed sufficiently serious to be reported, so the new exhibitor need not fear that innocent breaches of etiquette resulting from inexperience will bring down the full weight of officialdom on their heads.

The first thing to know is that exhibitors should not address the judge unless he specifically invites them to. This is to protect the impartiality and objectivity of the judge. Many judges will tell tales of some exhibitor or other who whispers such comments as, 'I was so pleased when my dog won Best in Show last week,' or 'He only needs one more Challenge Certificate to gain his title.' It goes without saying that the judge will ignore such remarks, but justice has to be seen to be done.

Politeness to judges and stewards is an absolute requirement and, however disappointed you may feel if results have not favoured you, common courtesy must prevail. Of course, you will naturally prefer the company of some exhibitors to others, but whilst in the ring you must ensure that your feelings are not apparent. However, do not be afraid of showing that you are enjoying the experience. By all means chat to those standing next to you, but try not to allow your concentration to wander too far from the main task. I know that I speak for many fellow judges when I say that I appreciate a convivial atmosphere in the ring. No judge ever feels comfortable if the prevailing atmosphere is reminiscent of a dentist's waiting room.

It is of course natural for a winning exhibitor to feel elated, but hysterical outbursts of joy or punching the air in triumph may not enhance your reputation. Neither should you allow your disappointment at losing to be obvious. It may backfire, as it did on one memorable occasion when a seasoned exhibitor collected up her dog into her arms and purposefully marched the full length of the ring emitting disapproving snorts, before realizing that she had gathered up her skirt with her dog!

Shelties are extremely aware of the moods of their owners and, as the prime objective of your presence in the ring is to present your dog to his best advantage, the utmost importance must be given to his feelings. A downcast or apprehensive dog will never to able to project his virtues sufficiently well to catch the eye of the judge, so it is vital that you approach the task in a positive and relaxed frame of mind. This is doubly important when showing youngsters who are starting out on their show careers, as the dog's early impressions will affect his attitude in the future.

Some very successful exhibitors might say that their dogs perform better if they show them only the minimum of attention in the ring, or

133

that talking to the dog can have a detrimental, rather than beneficial, effect. My personal opinion is that the reverse is true. Dogs benefit from encouragement and reassurance just as humans do, and one of my joys, when judging or exhibiting, is to see a handler relaxed and happy, with a dog who is showing his joy with that very slow and gentle tail-wagging so typical of our breed.

Awards

For each class, a judge selects the first-prize winner, the second, third and Reserve (fourth), and occasionally a Very Highly Commended

Austral. Ch. Nigma Gaius, owned and bred by Barbara and Jeff Phillips, Australia.

Ch. Beckwith Bit of a Glama Girl, owned and bred by Cath and Dave MacMillan.

(VHC, or fifth). When all the classes for males have been completed, the first-prize winners who have not been beaten in any other class return to the ring, where the judge selects the Best Dog. The same procedure is used to select Best Bitch. These two compete for the Best of Breed award. Puppies compete separately, and the Best Puppy is chosen in the same way.

At championship shows, the judge can award CCs (Challenge Certificates) to the Best Dog and Best Bitch if he considers them of outstanding merit. A dog that wins three CCs under three different judges is known as a Champion (Ch.). A Reserve CC can also be awarded, which is upgraded to CC if the original CC is disqualified for any reason. Dogs who win their titles in more than one country earn the right to be called International Champion (Int. Ch.).

135

The winners of CCs and Reserve CCs automatically earn an entry in the Stud Book, published by the Kennel Club each year, as do the first three dogs and bitches placed in limit and open classes. The Stud Book also shows the holders of the Junior Warrant, awarded to dogs and bitches who have scored points by winning specified prizes before they are eighteen months old.

The award systems in Scandinavia and mainland Europe are similar to the British. The Irish, American, Australian, and New Zealand Kennel Clubs have a totally different system, whereby the title of champion is awarded on a variable points system that takes into consideration the number of dogs entered at the show.

The immediate, tangible rewards of showing are rather meagre in Britain. There are rosettes for class winners, and larger rosettes for higher honours. Cups and other trophies are awarded at club shows, for the winner to keep until the next show. The prizes awarded in Scandinavia and elsewhere often look much more impressive. However small the prizes, most exhibitors take them home and give them pride of place. Only the most confident beginners think that the first rosette will be just one of many, but eventually your wall could be covered with a multi-coloured swathe of ribbon. If you are totally committed, and lucky as well, a special cabinet for your trophies could become yet another expense you never foresaw on the day when someone said 'What a beautiful Sheltie. You should show him.'

7

Judging

The responsibilities of a judge go beyond picking the winners of the day. A judge's decisions can have a profound effect on the development of a breed, because breeders and other enthusiasts are inevitably influenced by show results and the judges' reports that are published after shows. Good judging ensures that Sheltie breeders work to the Breed Standard; poor judging has the potential to change the breed out of all recognition.

Selection of Judges

The selection of judges used to be an opaque procedure, and mistakes were undoubtedly made. In order to improve selection, in 1980 the committee of the English Shetland Sheepdog Club embarked on a programme of training and assessing potential championship show judges, having studied a similar scheme introduced by the Southern Afghan Club. After some teething problems, the Training of Judges Scheme now has almost universal approval. The Mid Western Shetland Sheepdog Club, which had actively supported the scheme, became co-organizers and administrators of the scheme, and it has been extended to include non-specialists.

At the time of writing, the Kennel Club is considering adopting a similar scheme for all breeds. It is likely that in future new judges will be approved only if they have successfully completed the training course for a particular breed, or already appear on the official judges lists compiled by the breed clubs. It may also be that candidates will have to apply to be included on the judging lists, rather than wait to be invited (as they are now). In Great Britain, the breed clubs are at present almost equally divided between those that ballot their members to choose judges for their shows, and those in which a committee makes the decision. All of the general dog societies select judges by committee vote.

Training

The current training of Sheltie judges consists of lectures by breed experts, followed by a written examination to assess candidates' knowledge of the Breed Standard, and a practical examination, in which they judge dogs in front of a panel of breed experts. Given that the individual has sufficient judging experience, success in the Training of Judges Scheme will earn the candidate the support of the Breed Council when applying for the right to award Challenge Certificates. This training and assessment procedure is proving to be successful and is unlikely to be radically changed, although a way should perhaps be found to take account of 'exam nerves', which can paralyse even the most able candidate. Formal training is only one aspect of learning, and learning does not finish when formal training ends. The best and most experienced judges admit that they never cease to hone and develop their skills.

Swed. Ch. Shepherds Abcint, an early Swedish champion, by Helensdale Lorne out of Helensdale Donna.

Judging a Show

Assuming that you have the training and experience, you may be invited to judge a show. The Kennel Club has precise rules on how an invitation to judge is issued and processed, and takes action against transgressors. An informal invitation at the ringside or by telephone is not a formal contract to judge, but merely an enquiry about availability. The secretary of a club or society must send you a formal letter stating the date, type and venue of show, and the sex or sexes of the dogs to be judged. You should reply in writing to accept the invitation, but only when the secretary writes again confirming your acceptance is there deemed to be a formal and valid contract. Only in exceptional circumstances will the Kennel Club agree to your withdrawal from the appointment. Use the time before the show to refresh your knowledge of the Breed Standard.

What to Wear

A well-dressed judge inspires confidence and adds significantly to the occasion. You should look neat, but your clothing and footwear must also be comfortable and appropriate for the weather. Judging involves a lot of standing, walking and bending. High heels are awkward for outdoor shows, and too noisy for indoor events, as are heavy shoes. Large hats and flowing clothes are impractical, especially for outdoor shows, and may alarm the dogs. Long fingernails and jewellery are potentially dangerous when you are examining a dog's mouth. Wear a tie by all means, but use a tie-clip to stop it from flapping into a dog's eyes. Be sparing with scent and aftershave: dogs have sensitive noses.

Final Preparations

Equipment for the day should include the original invitation, with the time, date and venue, and any passes you have been sent for the carpark and show. Take two pens (one is a spare, in case of failure), preferably ballpoint to prevent your writing becoming smudged or washed out by rain. You must have a notebook, in which to write your critiques of first and second in each class, or a pocket tape recorder equipped with fully charged batteries. The day before the show, check your car thoroughly and fill up the fuel tank. Be sure you know exactly how to reach the venue, and allow plenty of time for the journey. You should reach the show venue at least forty-five minutes before judging is scheduled to start.

At the Show

On arrival, report immediately to the show secretary. You will be offered coffee and biscuits and given a folder containing your judging book and badge. It is useful at this point to check the number of dogs entered in each class, to estimate the time each class should take. You will carry out your task far more efficiently if judging proceeds at a steady, comfortable pace. The Kennel Club recommends that judges spend two minutes on each exhibit, but it has also ruled that one person can judge up to 250 dogs of a single breed in a day at a championship show, which means that you may have even less than two minutes per dog.

Find your ring and meet your stewards, who should already be at the judging table checking the contents of the box containing the awards. Walk around the ring to check for anything that might cause problems. A dog of mine once injured his foot on broken glass in the ring, and this was at Crufts.

Spectators and exhibitors will be arriving at the ringside by now. Expect to be ignored by the exhibitors, even those who would normally greet you effusively. Perhaps no one wishes to be seen seeking favour with the judge.

The stewards are there to arrange and control the ring under your direction. If you tell them your preferences for the positioning of the dogs to be judged, they will see that the exhibitors comply. Stewards deal with all queries from exhibitors, leaving you to concentrate fully on judging, and should involve you only in the most extreme cases. They are also empowered to draw your attention to any suspected incidents of double handling, and should enforce the Kennel Club rule that only the show manager, authorized people and exhibitors are allowed to enter the ring.

Judging

The pure mechanics of judging have been described many times, and I feel no useful purpose will be served by giving the details again. The object of judging is to compare each Sheltie to the Breed Standard. After briefly looking at all the dogs in the ring, the judge examines each dog on a table, and observes him as he moves in a triangle. There are no specific rules about how to proceed, but it is advisable to have a uniform and consistent routine. You can save time by not repeating actions. There is no need for detailed scrutiny when the dogs line up

Ch. Japaro Offbeat Jazz, owned and bred by Margo and Ian Nixon.

at the start of each class, as you will do a final assessment at the end, before placing the dogs. At the start, a walk up and down the ring is enough to give you a general impression of the class, and for any dogs of quality to make an impact.

Decide on the placings before bringing your winners into the centre of the ring, where your stewards will position them in accordance with Kennel Club rules. The highest-placed dog should be on the left (your left). You will look very unprofessional and indecisive if you change

your mind about placings at this point, and any revision usually causes resentment among the deposed. If you wish to pick out several dogs
for further consideration, be sympathetic to the feelings of the
exhibitors and do not pick out five when only four awards will be
made. It will also look odd if you pick out most of the dogs in the class.

There is an art to letting exhibitors know that you have placed their
dogs. My method is to touch the winners lightly on the arm in turn,
starting with the first-prize winner, and to tell them which placing I
have decided on. Some judges give an airy wave of the hand, but as an
exhibitor I have misunderstood this on a number of occasions and con-
fidently stepped forward, only to suffer the acute embarrassment of a
lonely trudge back to the line. Note the placings in your judging book
after each class, showing any withheld awards, and initial the tear-off
sections of the book.

The Kennel Club empowers judges to withhold awards from all
exhibits of insufficient merit, but remember that if a third place is not
awarded no subsequent placings can be made. The high quality of
Sheltie exhibits means that judges very rarely withhold awards. Lack
of quality is the only allowable reason for doing so. Some exhibitors
argue that the judge is required only to place the dogs in order of com-
parative merit, and that even if the quality of the class is not high, there
will always be one dog that is better than another.

The Judge's Critique

Before the next class begins, use your notebook or tape recorder to
make a few comments on your placed dogs. Every judge is expected
to submit a written critique on the first- and second-placed dog in each
class, giving the reasons for the placings. Sadly, a number of judges do
not carry out this time-consuming task, which means that their decisions are unexplained. Some societies quite correctly insist on a written critique as a condition of appointment. A well-written, informative
critique is of immense value to anyone assessing the current strengths
and weaknesses in the breed. The brief notes that you make at the
show should be detailed enough for you to write up a more elaborate
report when you return home.

Sheltie judges have good examples to follow, such as the remarkably
informative critiques of Albert White, founder of the Sharval kennel.
His direct style and astute observations made it quite clear why a particular dog was placed. The respected all-rounder Bobby James had a

gift for succinct and straightforward reasoning, coupled with an instinctive appreciation of type and soundness. Mary Davis, of the Monkswood Shelties, had a wonderful knack for word pictures that brought every dog to life.

All of these writers made critique-writing look easy. In fact it is difficult, but like all other skills it can be improved with practice and application. A judge need not be a literary genius, and brevity is desirable. The better critiques give a general description of the dog, (glamorous sable, correctly coloured merle, or whatever), followed by brief details of his outstanding features. It is useful if you mention failings, particularly when you are comparing with higher-placed dogs, but be sure that the dog actually has any fault or good quality that you attribute to him. Critiques must always be frank and honest but never brutal. Damning a dog in print is cruel and does a judge no credit, as readers wonder why the dog was placed, if his faults were so serious.

Int. Ch. Moorwood Classic Touch, the only dual British and Scandinavian champion, owned by Carin Ackeson and bred by B. and P. Svarstaad. (Photo. Dalton.)

Judging Overseas

The Kennel Club has a reciprocal agreement with the Fédération Cynologique Internationale (FCI), which governs dog breeding and showing in mainland Europe, including Scandinavia. This means that judges who are approved to award CCs in Britain are automatically approved for appointments in FCI countries. Those who have been honoured by an invitation to judge in other countries have always enjoyed great courtesy and hospitality. There are differences in judging protocol, but care is always taken to explain these.

Under FCI rules, every exhibit is awarded a grade by the judge, either as a number (1 to 4), or in words (Excellent, Very Good, Good, or Moderate). Every exhibitor receives a written critique on his dog before leaving the ring. The judge provides this by dictating a report

Int. N. S. Ch. Leeland Ring-around-Rosy, by Bannoch, owned and bred by Mr and Mrs H. Lie.

Austral. Ch. Hillacre Heavenly Blue, owned and bred by Robyn and Wally Courtnage, Australia.

on the spot to a ring secretary, who also ensures that the correct grade is awarded, in the form of a coloured ribbon.

When each exhibit in the class has been graded, the stewards call back into the ring all the Grade 1 (Excellent) exhibits, and the judge then places them first, second, and so on. There are additional awards for exhibits of outstanding merit, with Honour Prizes for puppies and Certificate Quality for adults. CCs are awarded to the winner of the open classes in which all Grade 1 dogs can compete. Some countries have a rule that a CC cannot be awarded to a dog under one year old. Champion dogs are exhibited in their own special class and cannot be awarded a CC, but may win Best of Sex over the CC winner. This is a useful rule in a breed like the Sheltie that is strong in both numbers and quality. As things stand in Britain, some excellent Shelties are simply not exhibited regularly. And, arguably, multiple CC-winners can prevent other dogs of outstanding merit from attaining a well-deserved title.

A particular feature of FCI shows is the informal gathering at the close, when exhibitors may ask you (most politely in virtually every case) about the qualities and faults that impressed you the most. In Britain judges used to walk around the benching area, chatting to the exhibitors, but have gradually stopped doing so. I regret this, because it is a sociable and useful way to end a show.

Integrity

As a judge, you are under the close scrutiny of your fellow Sheltie-breeders and exhibitors. At the end of the day, some of the losers will have a poor opinion of your judging ability, and some of the winners will think you are the best judge ever (on this day at least). You did not enter the ring to win friends, or placate enemies. You were asked to judge, not only because of your knowledge of the breed but because it was thought you would do so completely honestly and impartially. A judge very often has friends among the exhibitors, but is expected and required not to be influenced by this. Most judges try very hard to judge the dogs regardless of their handlers, and some judges are so anxious not to be charged with favouritism that they go too far, and do not reward the real merit in dogs handled by friends. Having said this, a few judges give awards to undeserving dogs to please friends or ingratiate themselves. One way to deal with these timewasters is to boycott them at their next show.

8

Breeding

A few breeders are very fortunate and achieve wonderful results at their first attempt. Far more have to wait longer for success, and some become disillusioned. You may hear grumblings at the ringside to the effect that new breeders are excluded from winning, or that only established breeders ever win. The truth is that breeding consistently good dogs takes years of hard work. A breeder must have thorough knowledge of lines and families, and does not acquire this overnight. Someone who has spent half a lifetime breeding Shelties is not guaranteed success, but is more likely to produce winners than a novice.

Breeding Shelties is not straightforward. Establishing the breed was a struggle (*see* Chapter 1), and it is still easier to breed poor Shelties than good ones, although the endeavours of the early pioneers mean that retaining type is less of a problem today. The would-be breeder should start by getting as much information as possible. Sheltie enthusiasts are fortunate in that there are several useful books on the breed, written by breeders with long experience. These and other successful breeders are usually willing to share their knowledge and experience. Producing healthy, sound and typical Shelties is a collective as well as an individual responsibility, and most of those involved with the breed recognize that sharing knowledge can only improve it. Beware the self-appointed experts who may have little more knowledge and experience than you, however. Their freely given advice may do more harm than good.

Inherited Defects

While early breeders juggled with the barely understood concepts of dominant and recessive genes, they were nevertheless blissfully unaware of inherited diseases and abnormalities. The modern breeder still has to wrestle with the genes, but has the extra responsibility of breeding dogs free from the various inherited defects that are identified with alarming frequency. Some distressing conditions are hereditary, and careful breeding helps to eliminate them. In the future, it may be commonplace to test a dog's DNA to find out if he carries any of the genes associated with particular conditions and should therefore not be used for breeding. If this happens, it will be interesting to see whether genetic testing improves the breed, or on the contrary reduces the number of dogs available for breeding so much that inbreeding or even crossing to other breeds becomes inevitable. Although some conditions definitely have a genetic origin, with others it is not clear whether genes or other factors are responsible.

Progressive Retinal Atrophy

Progressive Retinal Atrophy (PRA), or night blindness as it was once known, is an inherited condition in which the blood vessels bringing oxygen to the retina (at the back of the eye) gradually die. PRA leads inevitably to loss of vision. It was found that PRA in Shelties followed easily understood patterns of inheritance, and so it was relatively simple for breeders to exclude affected dogs from breeding programmes. So successful have British breeders been that PRA is no longer a problem among British Shelties.

Collie Eye Anomaly

The same cannot be said for Collie Eye Anomaly (CEA). CEA is said to be diagnosable in six-week-old puppies. Affected puppies do not deteriorate, and some shake it off completely, with no signs of CEA at later examinations. When the condition is severe it is known as columboma, and may lead to detachment of the retina. Retinas become detached for other reasons, however, and all the available information suggests that columboma causes it to happen in only a minute number of cases.

In the late 1960s, up to 70 per cent of all Shelties tested were thought to be affected by CEA. Alarmed by these findings, breeders almost universally tried to eliminate the condition, although there were insufficient data for veterinary experts to be certain how it was passed down through the generations. The assumption that a simple inheritance factor was responsible is now known to have been mistaken, but at least the warnings of wholesale blindness afflicting the breed have not been fulfilled.

Some breeders abandoned suspect bloodlines, in the hope that CEA would disappear. This did not happen, and although a growing number of dogs are thought to be genetically clear of CEA, breeders are still no closer to finding a lasting, complete answer to the problem. An added complication is disagreement among vets over diagnosis. In one Scandinavian country, breeders initiated a CEA seminar with many vets, who examined several dogs and gave alarmingly different opinions.

Hip Dysplasia

In the most serious form of hip dysplasia (HD), the head of the femur (thigh) dislocates from the socket in the pelvis. It is a serious problem in some of the larger and heavier breeds, but smaller breeds with low body weights, including Shelties, have comparatively few problems. In its most serious form, the condition usually manifests itself only in later life, when muscles and ligaments become weaker and fail to hold the head of the femur in place. There are three main causes of HD. Firstly, it may be hereditary, in which case the condition is passed on to the puppy by one or both parents. Secondly, it may be caused by excessive wear on the head of the femur or the socket, or both, usually brought about by a puppy having too much exercise before the bones have become sufficiently hard and strong. The third cause is dietary imbalance, resulting in poor or deformed bone structure. Few owners will admit to poor rearing or over-exercising youngsters, so practically every reported case is said to have been inherited. Usually the stud-dog is blamed, but this is quite unfair.

It seems that HD is present to some degree in all breeds except the Greyhound. The condition can be diagnosed from an X-ray of the hip, usually taken while the dog is anaesthetized, so that the leg can be stretched back to show any imperfections in the joint. The X-ray is analysed and given a score. Low scores mean that a dog is unlikely to show any outward signs in later life, whereas dogs scored higher may show signs of lameness or even suffer displacements. Many Sheltie breeders are understandably concerned by this method, given the well-documented intolerance to anaesthetic shown by some Shelties. It is not necessarily helpful either, as dogs with low scores do not always produce offspring with low scores, and high-scoring dogs do not automatically produce high-scoring puppies. Such is the complexity of the inherited form of HD that many breeders believe that the X-ray and scoring system is no real guide to the choice of breeding stock, and may result in the condensing of the existing gene pool, with dire consequences. Dogs that are severely affected by HD need not live in pain. A hip renewal operation has been perfected, with astounding results. It involves removing the head of the femur, and grafting bone on to the pelvis.

Genetics

All breeders have a responsibility to produce typical animals who are sound in body and mind. Knowledge of the assets and failings of the ancestors of breeding dogs is invaluable, which means plunging into the complicated world of genetics. You do not have to become an expert on genes to breed dogs, but it helps to know something about them. Many of the text books on genetics seem to have been written by and for only those who already thoroughly understand the subject. Other readers may be baffled and demotivated by the end of the first paragraph. I am indebted to Dr Dina Mobbs, an acknowledged expert in genetics and a close friend for many years, for the following guide.

Genes

A typical animal resembles its parents more than it resembles unrelated individuals, yet they are not identical. The similarities and differences between generations can be explained by the transmission of units called genes. The science of genetics is the study of genes through their variation and the transfer of information from one generation to the next. The outcome of crosses between individuals carrying differences (both plant and animal) has been the main approach to the study of genetics.

Practical genetics has gone on for thousands of years, in the form of selective plant and animal breeding, but the science of genetics is relatively new. Classical genetics originated in the 1870s with the experiments using garden peas carried out by an Austrian monk, Gregor Mendel. Although Mendel knew nothing of genes, his experiments identified factors that he postulated must be transmitted from parents to offspring. Discovery of the chemical nature of genes led to the new field of molecular genetics, with rapid advances in the 1950s and 1960s. Gene manipulation techniques only became widely used in the 1980s.

Chromosomes and Alleles

A gene is the principal unit of heredity and is composed of deoxyribonucleic acid, commonly known as DNA. A chromosome is formed

Five generations of Lythwood champion dogs. From left: *Ch.
Lythwood Saga, Ch. Lythwood Spruce, Ch. Lythwood Scrabble,
Ch. Lythwood Steptoe, and Ch. Lythwood Brandy Snap* (in front).

from thousands of genes in a long, continuous length of DNA. The
DNA from all the chromosomes together forms a complete blueprint
for the structure and function of the body. Humans have forty-six
chromosomes (twenty-three pairs), while dogs have seventy-eight
chromosomes (thirty-nine pairs).

Dogs (and humans) inherit one of each pair of chromosomes from
the mother and one from the father. Each chromosome of a pair should
contain the same sequence of genes in the same order but usually as
different versions known as alleles. The number of chromosomes and
the actual gene locations are constant for all breeds of dog, but there is
an enormous diversity of alleles. In a single breed a particular allele is
often present at a significantly higher or lower frequency than in the
species as a whole.

Genotype and Phenotype

The genotype is what a dog inherits from a previous generation: it is a
description of the alleles it carries for a given gene. The phenotype is
the visible or measurable effect of that underlying genotype: among
other things, it is what a dog looks like. The genotype remains con-

Willow Tarn Thimble (left) *with her sire Ch. Springcrest Lucky Titus from Willow Tarn, owned by Mrs R. Crossley.*

stant, but the phenotype changes, as the inherited genes interact with the environment. Two puppies that are genetically identical may develop differently in different environments, and two puppies that look similar may have different genotypes.

Single Gene Inheritance

The simplest form of inheritance is where one gene influences one trait. The puppy inherits an allele from its mother and an allele from its father for this trait. If one allele is called A and the other is called a, the pair received by the puppy may be AA, Aa or aa. When both alleles are of the same type (AA or aa) the dog is said to be a homozygote for that trait. When the two alleles are different (Aa), the dog is called a heterozygote. If this is a gene for coat colour, then what the Aa dog actually looks like (its phenotype) depends on the dominance pattern of the alleles. If the 'A' allele is completely dominant over the 'a' allele, then the 'Aa' dog will look the same as an 'AA' dog. The 'a' allele is said to be recessive. This is why traits sometimes skip a generation – if the dog mates with another 'Aa' dog, they may produce an 'aa' puppy which looks different from its parents. A recessive trait appears only when the allele is present in a homozygous state, or double dose. Two 'AA' dogs will breed true for that trait, and so will two 'aa' dogs, but the results of breeding with an 'Aa' dog are unpredictable.

The dominant-recessive relationship does not apply to all genes. Some alleles show co-dominance or partial dominance. To further complicate matters, some traits can be passed on only by females. This is known as X-linked inheritance, because it results from the fact that females have two X-chromosomes (XX), and males have one Y-chromosome and one X-chromosome (XY).

Polygenic Inheritance

The simplest form of inheritance, described above, is where one gene influences one trait and the resulting characteristic is easily identified. Nature is rarely that simple! Most phenotypes result from many genes. Although each of the contributing genes may act in the manner described, many different genes act on a single trait to create a continuous range of types. Often if two opposites are bred, the offspring have an intermediate phenotype. You then have to consider the effects of the environment (for example, diet and disease). Genes control the development of every characteristic but the final measurable variation from individual to individual is not necessarily the result of genetic variation alone. Characteristics such as height, weight, shape, colour, reproductive rate and behaviour vary more or less continuously.

The study of polygenic traits is called quantitative genetics and involves complex statistical analyses. For practical purposes, if dogs are selected for breeding because of some trait they have in common, the heritability is greater. This means that the trait is more likely to appear in the next generation than in the population as a whole.

Selective Breeding

Selective breeding changes the frequency of the alleles in a population. If dogs with a similar desirable trait are selected, the alleles that produce it will tend to become more common and, with luck, undesirable genes will be eliminated. In this way breeders significantly alter the gene pool – the alleles that are available. Breeders carry out a compressed and much faster version of the evolutionary process that Darwin identified. He recognized that natural selection takes place because some traits are more favourable than others. Differences arise through natural gene mutation: if a mutation results in a favourable trait, individuals that have it are more likely to reproduce and pass it on to the next generation. The accumulation of new alleles and changes in allele frequency result in new subgroups and species.

By careful observation and selective breeding, dog breeders have created breeds with remarkable breed-specific differences over approximately 150 years. While natural selection favours genes that confer some benefit for survival and reproduction, artificial selection focuses on traits deemed desirable by the selector. Originally breeders developed dogs to perform specific tasks.

The obvious way to develop strains with desirable traits is to find individuals with those traits and breed from them. This is effective for traits with high heritability, which means that you must study a dog's pedigree and look for evidence of the trait there. If the trait appears strongly among the dog's ancestors, then your plans are much more likely to work. There is no point in trying to breed for a trait that is caused by the dog's environment rather than its genes.

Inbreeding

Inbreeding is the mating of relatives, but in dog breeding it means the mating of very close relatives such as brother and sister or parent and offspring. The dogs breed more and more true, but undesirable genes may be inherited and fixed along with the desirable ones. Defects are not actually created by inbreeding, but hidden ones are almost certain to appear.

Ch. Ceirrhig Cragsman, owned and bred by Pat and Martin Griggs.

Many people find the thought of inbreeding rather abhorrent, because of the taboos and moral restrictions that are placed upon it in human society. The view that any mating between related individuals is inherently unsound because it is bound to result in flawed or deformed offspring is one of the arguments most frequently put forward by detractors of pedigree-dog breeding. And yet wild dogs, as well as feral domestic dogs for that matter, will naturally inbreed far more intensively than the majority of dog breeders would ever consider to be acceptable. In wolf packs, the dominant male has an inbuilt drive to spread his genes as widely as possible, and fathers all the cubs born within the pack for as long as his strength allows him

155

to fight off rivals, his own sons included. Closer to home, most cities and towns contain a population of dogs whose owners allow them to roam at will. The dominant male in the neighbourhood may mate with his own daughters if they are among the other dogs wandering loose, and his physical and mental characteristics consequently become very apparent in the population.

The attraction of inbreeding is that the offspring inherit all the good attributes shared by both parents, and bear a striking resemblance to them. Champions have been produced by this method, and it can be a quick way to establish a recognizable type. Without the intensive inbreeding carried out by the early pioneers of the Sheltie, we would probably not have the lovely dogs of today, but it condensed the gene pool considerably. Little fresh blood has officially been introduced since, and this means that inbreeding may carry a higher risk. Few serious breeders would use it today.

Outcrossing

Breeding unrelated dogs is known as outcrossing, and may seem a safer way to ensure that sound, healthy stock is produced. Breeders use outcrossing only with great care, because it is impossible to predict with any degree of accuracy how the puppies will turn out, physically or mentally. A breeder may occasionally introduce an unrelated individual into an established line, in the hope that specific attributes will be inherited by the puppies. Sometimes this produces spectacularly good results; more often the puppies have resembled neither parent. Continued outcrossing inevitably results in progeny that deviate wildly from the breed type in both looks and personality.

Line-breeding

Line-breeding is a loose term for the mating of dogs that are related, but not as closely as for inbreeding. The mating of cousins and second cousins is typical, although line-breeding might also include mating a dog with one of its grandparents. Line-breeding is a tried and trusted method of ensuring that breed characteristics are retained, because it consolidates the genes known to be present in the related animals, while different genes are introduced in small amounts. The mating of half-brother to half-sister also falls into this category, as despite the close relationship, each brings fresh genes from the unshared parent. Breeders use line-breeding to minimize unpredictable results.

Choosing a Mate

A breeder aims to produce puppies that conform as closely as possible to the ideal set out in the Breed Standard. This means that your bitch should be a good specimen with no major faults, and should be healthy and well exercised. When looking for a mate for your bitch, study both her pedigree and that of any stud-dog you are considering. Find out all you can about both dogs' families: watch their relations in the ring, talk to other breeders, and read all you can about Shelties and their bloodlines. Look at your bitch impartially, and try to identify any minor faults that you would prefer the puppies not to have. Look for a well-balanced stud-dog that has no major faults. If your bitch is a product of careful breeding, use the line-breeding technique and choose a stud-dog accordingly.

Int. Ch. Shelfrect Stroller, an influential Swedish stud-dog.

Contact the owner of the stud-dog of your choice before your bitch actually shows physical signs of season, to check that the owner will accept your bitch to be mated. The stud-owner is not obliged to accept any bitch, and may have legitimate concerns, based on experience, about the advisability of the proposed mating. Stud-owners should have scruples that will prevent them from allowing a dog to be used in an unsuitable mating.

The Right Time for Mating

Oestrus, known more commonly as a bitch's season or heat, may first occur when your bitch is six to eight months old, and usually recurs about every six to eight months thereafter. It is not unusual for the first season to be delayed until your bitch is a year old or even slightly older. Inexperienced owners may miss the season altogether if the bitch has what is called a 'silent season', in which there are no obvious visible signs.

When your bitch is about to come into season, you may notice that she urinates away from home much more frequently. She is actually leaving her scent to advertise her condition to prospective partners. Her behaviour may also change: she may become much more active and animated, and show you even more affection than usual. It is possible with experience to notice a change in the facial expression of some bitches, whose eyes assume a quite different and unmistakable sheen. A bitch may also approach you wagging the whole of her body and panting, even though she has not exerted herself. Her vulva may start to swell at this time, though some never noticeably enlarge, and you may observe a slight brownish discharge. More licking than usual of the vulva should alert you to the change in a bitch's status.

The first day of the season proper is counted from when the discharge changes to an obvious blood red, although Shelties, especially older bitches, are often meticulous in cleaning themselves whilst in heat and you will miss this change unless you are extremely vigilant. Seasons usually last for three weeks, and the flow of blood may be more copious during the first seven to ten days. Some bitches do not seem to be sexually attractive to male dogs at this stage, but others appear to be irresistible to males from the first day. Do not be tempted to allow your bitch to associate with dogs now, even if they apparently show no interest. A Sheltie kept as a pet should not be exercised away from home. Every hopeful male in the neighbourhood will follow her scent to your

158

Int. Nord. Ch. Mondurle's Bannoch, sire of twenty-two champions,
imported to Norway from England by Mr and Mrs Helge Lie.

door and sit in hopeful and often not so silent anticipation, advertising his presence by urinating against your gatepost.

After the tenth day, your bitch enters 'oestrus', when eggs are released from the ovaries, and she begins to emit a strong scent that excites the male. She may also stop bleeding and start to produce a clear discharge. Many owners believe that this signifies the end of the season and allow the bitch to resume a normal life, with disastrous consequences! It is at this time that a bitch is at her most fertile and can be mated, often up to the eighteenth or nineteenth day. Some books advise mating the bitch on day ten, others on day twelve or day fourteen. Unfortunately Shelties do not read the books, and are not aware that they should be ready for mating on a particular day. Some bitches thought to be barren when mated early in oestrus have conceived when mated on the nineteenth or even twentieth day of their season. Conversely, bitches that fail to conceive at the normal time have become impregnated when mated at day five or six.

So when is the best time to mate your bitch to ensure that she will conceive? When she is ready seems a glib answer but is nevertheless true. The folklore about establishing the best time for mating is entertaining, but much of it is ludicrously inaccurate and misleading. There is a test available through your vet that accurately forecasts the correct date, from analysis of a swab taken from the vulva. This test is particularly useful for bitches with silent seasons, because the owner cannot even roughly forecast the right date if no coloured discharge is discernible, and you need a date in order to book a stud-dog. You can test a bitch yourself and get an immediate result using a kind of litmus paper, also available from the vet. Users of both tests find them reliable.

If a number of bitches are kept together, some form of flirtation and even mounting may occur when a bitch is in season. Such sexual behaviour is not a reliable guide to the correct time to mate a bitch, as it may predate the time when she is receptive to the dog by some days. A bitch may also flirt outrageously with a dog several days before she is ready to be mated.

The Mating

You will already have been in touch with the stud-owner and had your bitch accepted for mating. When you observe the first signs of season, telephone immediately to confirm the booking. This is vitally important, especially if your choice is a popular and well-used stud. In your own interests, give the date when you really think the bitch will be most fertile, not the date most convenient for you. It may be easier to travel with your bitch at the weekend, but do not be surprised if an unsuccessful mating is the result. Always telephone the day before you take your bitch to be mated, and ask the best time to arrive. Leave home in plenty of time to be punctual.

Tidy your bitch up before leaving home but, however fastidious you are, do not bathe her, especially not at the rear end, or you may wash away the aroma that the stud-dog finds irresistible. If possible find a place where your bitch can relieve herself before you arrive. She will certainly be less tense and should be more receptive to the dog if she has an empty bladder.

The stud-owner always supervises the mating process. The ritual developed through the years by some superstitious stud-owners may surprise you, but do try to remain passive. Any anxiety you feel will

Five Mohnesee champions. From left: *Ch. Sonymer Sorceress to Mohnesee, Ch. Mohnesee The Sorcerer, Ch. Mohnesee The Illusionist, Ch. Mohnesee Margarita and Ch. Faybars Mai Tai With Moines.*

be transmitted to your bitch, which may make the mating difficult, and the sounds of your barely suppressed laughter will not endear you to the stud-owner.

It is usual for the bitch's owner to be present, as this generally has a calming effect on the bitch, and satisfies the owner that the mating has taken place satisfactorily. Very occasionally a difficult bitch will become relatively placid if her over-anxious owner is removed. If you agree with the stud-owner that it might be best for you to go somewhere else, ask to be called back in order to see the successful mating under way.

You may read that the dog and bitch indulge in elaborate flirting and chasing games prior to coupling, but many bitches are more aggressive than playful when they meet the stud. It is asking too much of a bitch

'Shelties in the Norwegian mountains. From left: Nor. Ch. Sumburgh Witch Hazel, Cover Girl, N. S. Ch. Ellington Endow, Int. Nord. Ch. Sumburgh Lulu Belle, Int. Nord. Ch. Ellington Early Riser, Nord. Ch. Ellington Exploder, and Nord. Ch. Midnightsun Talk of the Town, all owned by Mr and Mrs H. Lie.

to expect her to be keen about an enthusiastic stud, if she has only just got out of a car after perhaps several hours of driving. It may also happen that a bitch who seems very forward and appears to be enjoying the preliminaries, can suddenly object very strongly when the dog attempts penetration.

At our kennel, to avoid any unpleasant incidents we ask the bitch's owner to hold her in a close-fitting collar, with one hand on either side of her head. We then put one hand under the bitch's stomach, with the first and second finger on either side of her vulva to guide it in the direction of the male's thrusts. We hold the bitch's tail to the side with the other hand, but have never had to resort to tying her breechings in bunches, or more drastically cutting off most of the breechings, which used to be common practice.

When the dog penetrates fully, he clings even tighter to the bitch's hips, and invariably his tail curls significantly. His thrusts become more urgent and after a short time, he becomes still. This is the beginning of the stage called the 'tie'. A swelling occurs halfway along the dog's penis, and a ring of muscle in the bitch's vulva tightens to grip it. Semen begins to emit, not spurt, from the penis at this time, and is soon followed by a clear seminal fluid that allows the sperm to swim more freely. A tie does not always take place, and indeed is not needed for successful conception. Sometimes the dog does not penetrate far enough, particularly if the bitch is rather long cast and her muscle ring is correspondingly deeper inside. Some dogs never tie but still succeed in getting bitches in whelp.

However, many people feel strongly that the tie is very significant. To encourage a tie, we support the male's rear by putting an arm around him, and press him towards the bitch until we are fairly sure the tie has taken place. The bitch will often moan and cry while the tie is forming, and it is sometimes possible to feel her stomach muscles contracting. After a short while, the moaning and agitation will cease and it is then possible to allow the dog to move from the bitch's back, by letting his front legs come gently down onto the ground on one side of the bitch. If the tie is still complete, the dog may want to swing his hind leg over the back of the bitch to assume a rear-to-rear position. This position appears, incomprehensibly, to be more comfortable for the dog, and is a stance inherited from his wild forefathers, allowing them to face any attack from jealous rivals at a time of acute vulnerability.

A tie may last for a few seconds or up to forty-five minutes, or even longer in extreme cases, but the length of the tie does not appear to have any connection to the number of puppies produced. I once heard the celebrated vet Joan Joshua state in a lecture on fertility that dogs in her own breed (Chow Chow) rarely if ever tied. She attributed this to the rather aggressive behaviour of the female during the mating process. Lengthy ties are physically wearing for both dogs and owners. My worst experience was a one-hour tie that happened when I was mating my dog to a bitch in a secluded place beside a river one winter's evening, with snow on the ground and the temperature below freezing. The dog's ardour was not affected, but I was almost frozen to the ground.

You may encourage a tie to break by returning the dog to his first position, which eases the pressure of the bitch's muscles on the swelling in the dog's penis. This enables the trapped blood to flow back into the body of the male, and the swelling may reduce sufficiently in size for the penis to slide out easily. First lift the dog's hind leg and gently swing it over the back of the bitch so that they stand side by side, then lift the foreleg nearest to the bitch and place that over the back, making sure that you support the weight of the dog. Gently shove the dog's pelvis towards the bitch for a few seconds and await developments. It is not possible to force the breaking of a long tie without causing pain or discomfort to the dogs, and no form of encouragement other than the one described above should ever be attempted. Buckets of cold water may have a debilitating effect on humans, but have absolutely no effect on dogs.

Some breeders prefer bitches to be mated twice, with the matings forty-eight hours apart. If the bitch and the dog are both fertile, and if the bitch is presented at the correct time, there should be no need to mate more than once. If a bitch has failed to conceive after a satisfactory mating on a previous occasion, a second mating is a comforting reassurance. The owner of a bitch pays for the mating, not for conception, but only the meanest stud-owner would refuse to offer a free service to the same bitch at her next season should she not become pregnant.

Before you take your bitch home, the stud-owner should give you a completed Kennel Club certificate, to enable you to register the resulting offspring. You will also usually receive a copy of the stud-dog's pedigree to five generations. Ensure that your bitch does not come into contact with any other males until after her season is finished. Dual conception can and does take place.

9

Pregnancy and Whelping

The normal gestation period for dogs is sixty-three days, but many Shelties produce their puppies two or three days earlier. This tendency seems to run in certain families, and the puppies are usually born at acceptable birth weights of 6–8oz (170–227g). Our Ch. Rainelor Reinetta (Bramble) gave birth to two puppies ten days early. They weighed only 3oz (85 g) each, could not suckle, had no nails, and had only pink skin in the places where they should have had white fur. Bramble would do nothing for the puppies until they were three weeks old, and Patti hand-reared them. Despite the mother's neglect of duty, the puppies thrived and one became Ch. Hartmere Hello Gorgeous.

Pregnancy

To give birth and rear puppies successfully, your bitch must be as fit and well nourished as possible. Exercise is essential, but do not let her exercise freely with other dogs as collisions while running can have catastrophic results. Avoid any trauma and try to ensure that life is normal and undemanding. Taking the pregnant bitch on long journeys by car is not a good idea, nor is including her in family holidays, or sending her to stay with friends or in boarding kennels. Stress and strain can bring on abortion or the less obvious resorption in the womb, which is far more common than many people realize.

Some bitches take very good care of themselves. They adopt a more serious approach to life from day one, and this is usually the first sign of pregnancy. Others show little if any change in attitude, which is frustrating for all but the most patient owners, as they wait to see if mating has been successful. A slight vaginal discharge is another positive early indication of pregnancy, but three weeks into gestation is the earliest that abdominal palpation will reveal the presence of puppies. At this stage they are the size of marbles. Ultrasound scans can also detect pregnancy at this stage, although

Shelties usually have fairly small litters and the singleton puppy is sometimes difficult to detect.

There is no need to increase the volume of food until six weeks into the pregnancy, but from day one you should certainly feed easily digested protein such as fish and chicken, sometimes with cheese. A change of diet in the early stages may cause the bitch, worryingly, to refuse food. Any abstinence is usually very temporary and she will soon try to convince you that she is eating for sixteen puppies at least. After six weeks you can increase the amount of food considerably, but give it in two or more meals per day, as the pressure of puppies on the

Ceirrhig Controversy Reserve CC and CC winner, owned and bred by Pat and Martin Griggs.

166

digestive tract may limit the amount a bitch can eat at one time. A balanced diet that contains good-quality, easily digested protein should be sufficient for her needs, and supplements should be unnecessary. A calcium and phosphate supplement can be given for bone development if you need the reassurance that the bitch is getting everything she needs, but do be careful not to give too much of any supplement, as an excess can cause severe problems. If in doubt, be guided by your vet. The homoeopathic remedy *Caulophyllum* (6x potency) can be given during pregnancy, in order to ease the birth and help prevent complications. Some breeders give raspberry leaf herbal supplement, which is also considered to ease whelping.

The first visible indication of pregnancy appears at about five weeks, when a bitch's nipples become distinctly enlarged and pinker than usual. At this time, you may feel a slight swelling in the bitch's abdomen if you stand her with her front legs on a chair, so that her rib cage is stretched forward.

Preparations for Whelping

A bitch should get used to her whelping box two or three weeks before the puppies are due. It should be large enough for the bitch to stretch out in fully, away from her puppies, and should be accessible for the owner. Use a proprietary bedding that is safe for the puppies and easy to keep clean. Have a couple of spare pieces, because it will need frequent washing. We encourage our pregnant bitch to sleep in her whelping box, and bring it into our bedroom at night. Any other warm, quiet room where the bitch is relaxed will do as whelping quarters. A bitch can whelp in a kennel, but ensure that there is no distraction from other dogs. The very last thing you need is for your bitch to become anxious, as this can lead to complications. Warmth is essential, and the kennel should have an infra-red lamp with a dull emitter and wire guard.

You will also need plenty of newspapers and towels, sterilized scissors, and weighing scales, to record the birth weight. Even if you do not a believe in estimating full-grown size from birth weight, it is useful to check weights daily from birth to reassure yourself of the wellbeing of the puppies. Prepare a small cardboard box with a hot water bottle wrapped in a blanket at the bottom, to keep the first puppies warm whilst subsequent births are taking place. Also have glucose to hand, and a homoeopathic remedy, if you use them, in case a puppy is not very vigorous when born.

Signs of Imminent Whelping

Warn your vet several days before the birth is due, in case assistance is required. Most Shelties give birth quite naturally and easily, unlike some other breeds for which Caesareans are the normal practice. As the time to give birth approaches, many bitches revert strongly to nature and search for a quiet, dark, secluded place in which to have her puppies. Cupboards are often preferred, and major excavations under garden sheds and kennels can take place. It is not unknown for bitches to escape as they look for a more remote place for the birth, so do watch your bitch carefully as the date draws closer. Our bitches seem happy with our bedroom as a whelping quarters. Another advantage is that we are alerted to the first, and sometimes very brief, preliminaries of labour, when the bitch scratches up bedding to make a nest. Some bitches, rather maddeningly, start this process days before the birth, but it is often an indication that things are about to happen. As a precautionary measure, take the temperature of the bitch at regular intervals, from two days before you expect the puppies to be born. When temperature drops from the normal 100.5–101.5°F (38–38.6°C), to below 99.5°F (37.5°C), birth takes place within twenty-four hours.

Sommerville Seed Pearl (two CCs), owned and bred by Mr M. J. Ewing.

Owners whose dogs live in the family home may notice that for a period of time before contractions begin, a bitch has a dreamy, faraway look in her eyes, which is closely followed by unrest, and perhaps even slight trembling. Unless you are happy to have the puppies born on your best chair, now is the time to put the bitch in her whelping box.

The Whelping

In a normal birth, after several minutes of straining, a bitch arches her back and the first puppy is born. The dam should open the membrane bag, sever the cord and lick the puppy dry. Do not be alarmed if your bitch first passes a quantity of green liquid. This is fairly common, and is not a sign of impending trouble. Some bitches, even maidens, take complete charge of the birth and reduce you to an interested, nail-biting spectator. Others never seem to know what to do, and simply look at what they have produced. In this case open the bag and sever the cord. Some breeders tie off the cord at least an inch (2.5cm) from the puppy before cutting the cord with scissors; others simulate the action of the bitch's teeth by severing the cord with fingernails. In any case, hands and/or equipment must be scrupulously clean. Once the cord is cut the bitch will normally deal happily with the puppy.

The uterus of the dog has two horns that converge into one passage, and the contents of one horn are discharged before the other. Your bitch may, if you are lucky, give birth to her puppies at regular intervals over a relatively short space of time, or she may rest for up to half an hour between puppies. Any longer interval, if there are obviously more puppies to be born, should give rise to suspicions of possible internal problems. Occasionally there is a noticeable rest period after two or three puppies have been born, and this may be a natural break after one horn has emptied and before the other begins to expel puppies.

Weigh the puppies and record their weights as they are born, but handle them as little as possible. You may like to put puppies on the wrapped hot water bottle to keep them warm and clean as the other puppies are born.

Few bitches relax and feed puppies between births, and you can be pretty sure that the birthing process is over if a bitch settles down to nursing the litter. It is not a completely reliable sign: one of our bitches unexpectedly produced a puppy an hour after she had gone to sleep having cleaned and nursed her first four puppies.

169

Opinions are divided over whether to allow the bitch to eat the pla-centas. In a natural situation the bitch would be most reluctant to leave her puppies unattended in the early days, and the placentas might be the only nourishment available to her. Placentas do provide nourish-ment, and she should be allowed one, but eating too many can have a drastic laxative effect.

Whelping Complications

Most Shelties give birth remarkably easily, but occasionally complica-tions arise. One of the commonest problems is failure to continue con-tracting, after labour has started in textbook fashion. Vets may tell you that in theory a bitch can go for several days, without problems, between the first and second stages of labour, but it would be unwise to count on this. If there is no further progress two hours after the first contractions, call the vet. The bitch may need an injection of Oxytocin to stimulate the contractions. Usually puppies are born amazingly quickly after the injection – we have had births on the back seat of the car on the return journey from the surgery.

Caesarean Section

If an injection does not bring about the required result, your vet may advise a Caesarean section. There is always a risk with operations under anaesthetic, but to wait and see might be more dangerous for both puppies and bitch. It is not common for a Sheltie to require a Cae-sarean. She will be rather sleepy immediately after the operation, and the puppies may also be slightly affected by the anaesthetic. Check very carefully that they feed satisfactorily and are cleaned by the dam. We have had only one Caesarean birth, and the bitch went on to devel-op deep trauma symptoms. Initially she seemed to have no idea how to bond with the sole survivor, and as her resentment towards him grew, we had to remove him and hand-rear him. The bitch accepted him as soon as he was weaned, and gave us no further concern.

Postnatal Care

The heart-warming sight of your bitch, now safely delivered of her puppies, lying smugly in her box with puppies feeding contentedly,

170

Contentment. A litter of Lirren puppies, bred by Mrs Lynn French.

should not lull you into a false sense of security. Warmth is an obvious basic requirement for the well-being of mother and family, but too much warmth can soon bring on heat exhaustion and dehydration. If you have a heat lamp over the box, place it off-centre, so that the bitch can find a cooler position when she wants to.

You may be astonished by the voracious appetite of your bitch while she is nursing a litter. It is essential to give her an easily digested, high-protein diet, so that she can produce milk that is sufficiently rich to nourish the puppies. Give meat, fish (pilchards are particularly appreciated), scrambled eggs, and plenty of cereals, such as the unsweetened brands sold for babies. These can be mixed with goat's milk. You can also buy a complete food for nursing bitches, just as you can for every other stage of a dog's life. This will be quite adequate, but we prefer to offer a variety of foods to ensure that the bitch's appetite is stimulated and the free flow of milk uninterrupted.

Weigh the puppies daily for the first week to check that they are gaining weight. A hungry puppy cries all the time, with a thin quavering sound that is both distressing and alarming. The majority of

Shelties are excellent and attentive mothers, who suckle their puppies readily, clean up their faeces, and stimulate their digestive systems by licking their tummies.

Supplementary Feeding

Occasionally a bitch is a reluctant and indifferent mother, and may even abdicate all responsibility for her family. Supplementary feeding

Ch. Lirren Hasbrown aged eight weeks, owner and breeder Mrs Lyn French.

is necessary in this situation, or if the bitch has little or no milk, or if a puppy is too weak to feed itself. Hand-feeding is a harrowing and time-consuming chore. We use goat's milk, now readily available at supermarkets, as it contains almost as much fat and protein as a dam's milk. However, do try to ensure that puppies receive the colostrum contained in the early feeds from their mother, as it is rich in antibodies. It is easiest to use an eyedropper to feed a puppy. A feeder designed for premature babies is also effective, but you may have to enlarge the hole in the teat to make feeding easier. Tube-feeding involves inserting a plastic tube through the mouth and into the puppy's stomach. It is a delicate operation, and should not be attempted by the unqualified.

If the bitch does not lick the puppies' stomachs to encourage urination and defecation, use a piece of cotton wool soaked in olive oil to gently massage their tummies after every feed. It is unusual for a puppy to show signs of intolerance to goat's milk but, if it does, other fluids are vitally important to prevent dehydration. Glucose and boiled water are sustaining, and chicken essence is recommended by many as a suitably nourishing alternative to milk.

You may have to feed puppies hourly for a week or even longer. The strain on your mental and physical health will be severe, but the reward more than compensates, as you watch puppies that you have hand-reared grow into strong healthy adults.

Postnatal Complications

A Sheltie mother is usually extremely proud of her offspring, and seems to enjoy the regular visits you make to check on her and her family. This is just as well, as you need to check both dam and puppies frequently.

Mastitis

Check the bitch several times each day for any hardness in her teats, which could herald the onset of mastitis. Teats that are not used are most likely to be affected, as they become engorged with milk. Apply warm water fermentations liberally with a sponge for several minutes, at least three times daily for several days, to remove the hardness and restore the milk flow. *Urtica urens*, a homoeopathic remedy is also effective. If mastitis takes hold, the milk glands will become inflamed, and antibiotics may be needed.

Eclampsia

You must also check the bitch for signs of eclampsia (also called milk fever), which occurs when feeding the puppies imposes a strain on the bitch's reserves of calcium. It affects bitches who are nursing small litters as well as those with large ones. The symptoms are sudden and dramatic, and can strike at any time when the bitch is lactating, but are most often seen in the second week after birth.

The first indications of eclampsia are usually extremely rapid panting and a glazed expression in the bitch's eyes, often accompanied by uncontrollable trembling. The bitch becomes highly agitated and increasingly uncoordinated, often to the point of collapse, when her limbs will stiffen and she may convulse. A lapse into unconsciousness follows swiftly, and she may die in a very short space of time. It is imperative that you seek immediate veterinary assistance when you notice the first signs, whatever the hour of day or night, as the only treatment for the condition is a high dose of calcium administered intravenously (calcium supplements are ineffective).

Care of the Puppies

Nails and Dew-Claws

Cut the puppies' claws with nail scissors at least twice a week, or your bitch will be in severe discomfort from the constant scratching as the puppies palpate her to stimulate the milk flow. Be careful to remove only the hooked end portion of the claw, to avoid pain and bleeding. A bitch may be come anxious if one of her puppies squeaks during the manicuring, so we try to do it while the bitch is making a toilet excursion to the garden.

Very occasionally, Shelties are born with hind dew-claws, a relic of their ancestry. Dew-claws should be removed by the vet at two or three days, when the bone is still gristle. Dew-claws that are left can cause problems in later life when they become tangled in fabrics or are torn in exercise. Many years ago, the front dew-claws of Shelties were removed for the same reasons and also for cosmetic purposes. The front dew-claws seem to have been much larger then than they are now and few if any Shelties today have them removed. Accidents involving these claws are mercifully few if the nails are clipped regularly.

Socializing

Puppies are born with their eyes tightly shut and their ears closed, but they respond to touch from birth. We feel it is important to handle puppies as early as the dam feels comfortable with the intrusion. Between ten and fourteen days, the eyes start to open, often one eye before the other, which gives the puppy an endearing and comical appearance. Sounds also start to register, and the puppies soon learn to recognize your voice and tumble out of their box to greet you. Invariably the first thing they do on leaving the box is to urinate: spread paper in front of the box to facilitate house-training on paper at a later stage.

From now on, your life will not be your own. The puppies develop quickly and begin to play with each other, and with you. You will spend more and more time watching and handling them, but this is time well spent, as you are helping to form their characters and preparing them for the world outside. We are lucky enough to have many friends who are interested in the dogs and who come to see our puppies regularly as they are growing. It is all the better when they bring children (so long as the children are well behaved) to talk to the puppies and cuddle them, always on the floor to avoid wriggling puppies being dropped. This early socializing is very valuable, and equips most puppies with a life-long ability to adjust easily to other people.

Weaning

Weaning can start at three weeks. The first food for our puppies is usually but not always a rice pudding meal made with goat's milk and a little honey. Puppies differ considerably in their tastes, and many prefer to go straight for the meat. We use a proprietary puppy food mashed to a very soft consistency. Puppies start with one or two meals on the first day, and are soon eating two milk-based meals and two meat-based meals a day.

Meal times may appear to be totally chaotic, as puppies' table manners leave everything to be desired, and walking through food seems to be obligatory. There should be rules, however. We prefer to feed each puppy from a separate dish, and pick it up, with any food that is left, as soon as the puppy walks away. This is to discourage gluttony and fighting at feeding times, and to encourage fussy eaters to finish the whole meal at one sitting. Our puppies are eating a complete puppy food by the time they leave for other homes, which makes feeding a well-balanced diet easy both for us and for the new owners.

'Best foot forward'. A nine-week Glensanda bitch puppy, owned and bred by Mrs Sheila Powell.

As the puppies take more solid food, their reliance on the dam decreases, and they need not be with her all the time. Most bitches are only too pleased to relinquish nursery duties and return to a normal life. A dam might pop into the puppy pen only occasionally during the day, but still show a desire to sleep with the puppies at night. By the time the puppies are five weeks old, the bitch is usually happy to leave the puppies alone at night and, as her milk is drying up, is less than enamoured by puppies chasing after her to reach the milk bar.

Worming

Worming should be carried out at three weeks, five weeks and seven weeks. Wormers are available as liquid, tablets or granules. Pet shops sell them, but for peace of mind you should use one supplied by your vet. The liquid form is probably the easiest to administer to an unco-operative puppy. Whatever you use, ensure that the dose is correct for the weight of puppy. Separate the dam from the puppies for two hours or so after worming, and clear up the faeces before she has a chance to do so.

Going Out

The puppies are still far too young to be taken for walks or to meet other dogs. Any unavoidable contact with the outside world should be handled with care. Between six and seven weeks, an eye specialist can test puppies for CEA (*see* Chapter 8). If you are going to a veterinary surgery for this or any other reason, do not linger in the waiting room with your puppies, in case they pick up a virus or other infectious dis-ease. Arrange to go straight into the consulting room, where steriliza-tion is carried out after each patient leaves.

For our puppies, the eighty-mile drive to the eye specialist is their first long car journey. A single puppy can travel on a passenger's knee, but several puppies should travel in a crate. Place bedding in the bot-tom of the crate so that the puppies do not slip, and drive very care-fully to prevent their being thrown about.

Going to New Homes

The care and attention that you have lavished on the puppies should be evident in their physical appearance and mental well-being. Con-scientious owners are fully entitled to glow with pride as the puppies' new owners call, one by one, to collect their new companions. When the puppies leave to start their new lives, you will experience conflict-ing emotions: real sadness at the loss of an endearing little person whom you have grown to love, and happiness in the knowledge that he is leaving to give another home many years of love and joy.

10

Ailments and Diseases

Shelties are generally fit and robust dogs. We once said a last goodbye to a much-loved fifteen-year-old, and were surprised that the vet could not find her file, until we realized that she had not attended the surgery since her last litter, at four. Dogs of any breed may become unwell, however, even if they have the best of care.

A good relationship with your vet is essential. Unnecessary visits to the surgery should be avoided, but calling the vet sooner rather than later is sound advice when you are really concerned about the health of your dog. Conscientious owners know their dogs so well that they notice any changes in their well-being, however slight, and perhaps before any clinical symptoms are apparent. A good vet acknowledges this and reacts accordingly.

Temperature

An adult dog should have a temperature of 100.5–101.5°F (38–38.6°C). The temperature is taken with a rectal thermometer. This should not be tried by the inexperienced, as the thermometer might break – with disastrous consequences. It is very useful to know how to take a dog's temperature, however, and new owners should ask a vet or other expert to show them the technique.

Emergencies

Bleeding and Bruising

Shelties are rarely belligerent, and have the speed to run away from confrontations with other dogs, but occasionally a dog might be attacked by other dogs while exercising, or injured in some other way. Wash puncture wounds immediately with plenty of water containing antiseptic, and press a sterile pad onto the wound, using direct pressure. Any lacerations may need stitching by the vet. *Ledum* is a useful homoeopathic remedy. Bruising is less obvious, but some stiffness may alert you to the problem, and it is apparent when you touch the dog. Rest is the cure, although the homoeopathic remedy *Arnica* will speed the healing process.

Fractures

Dogs can break bones as easily and in the same variety of ways as humans can. Collisions with cars are often responsible. Reluctance to put body weight on a limb is an obvious sign that it may be broken, but broken ribs are less easy to diagnose. If a dog is involved in an accident, immobilize him as effectively as you can, and look for symptoms of shock. Go immediately to the veterinary surgery, where X-rays will be taken and treatment given. If your dog is fitted with a plaster cast, he should wear an Elizabethan collar (so called because of its resemblance to the ruffs of Elizabethan times), to prevent him from chewing through it.

Heat Stroke

People who leave a dog in a car on a sunny, not necessarily hot, day are committing an offence and should be prosecuted. It can cause heat stroke, as the temperature inside a stationary car rises remarkably quickly. Taking dogs for long, exhausting walks at the hottest part of a summer day is another cause. Immediate first aid is to reduce the dog's temperature as quickly as possible, either by immersion in water or by hosing down. Then take him to a vet. Heat stroke is a very serious condition, which can be fatal. Bear in mind, as well, that a heat-stroke victim is also likely to go into shock (*see* page 180).

Pyometra

All breeders fear this life-threatening uterine infection. Excessive licking of the vulva should alert you to the possibility of pyometra. Other signs are that a bitch drinks large amounts of water and has a high temperature. She may have a pussy discharge, but after a season the pus builds up in the uterus instead, because the presence of progesterone makes the cervix close. This is known as closed pyometra, and the owner may think the bitch's depression is caused by the season ending.

179

Immediate veterinary treatment is essential. If the infection does not respond to antibiotics, the uterus will have to be removed.

Poisoning

Most homes contain poisons in the form of household cleaning products, and some have deadly substances designed to eliminate vermin. Any potentially dangerous products for house or garden should be kept away from dogs. Puppies are especially at risk. The symptoms of poisoning are as varied as the poisons themselves. Some poisons cause profuse salivation, others rapid breathing, pupil shrinkage, convulsions, or coma. Call your vet immediately if you suspect poisoning. Treatment is far easier if you know what has caused the problem. A vet may struggle to treat your dog if the toxin is not identified.

Shock

Shock is a clinical condition, which can in itself be fatal. Injury, stress or other trauma such as heat stroke can cause a dog's nervous system to over-react. Signs of shock are an obvious and unnatural paleness of the gums, shivering, and a weak but rapid heartbeat. His eyes may appear glazed and his feet may be cold to the touch. Wrap the dog in something warm and seek veterinary help immediately. A small amount of whisky or brandy can be beneficial, as may be a few drops of Rescue Remedy (one of the Bach's Flower Remedies range, obtainable from chemists) on the tongue.

Stings

Catching bees and wasps in flight appears to be a particularly enjoyable pastime for Shelties, and it is surprising that they do not get stung more often. If a dog is pawing at his mouth or rubbing his face along the floor, examination may reveal the sting as an angry red swelling. A homoeopathic remedy is available, and gives almost instant relief.

Anal Glands

The anal glands are just inside the dog's rectum and are used to impart a lubricating coating to firm faeces. They can cause intense irritation if they become impacted, which happens when a dog's diet does not contain enough roughage to stimulate their operation. The glands can be emptied by squeezing the fluid-containing sacs, located either side and below the anus, until the compacted, foul-smelling core squirts out into a handily placed tissue. However, when inexpertly done this procedure can cause discomfort to the dog so you will need to have it demonstrated to you by an experienced person before attempting it yourself.

Arthritis and Rheumatism

Older dogs are often subject to these conditions. Arthritis attacks the joints, often at the site of an earlier, and sometimes very slight, injury. Rheumatism mainly affects the muscles and is largely non-attributable. It is often thought to be arthritis, and the symptoms of stiffening gait and difficulty in rising are virtually inseparable. Small doses of aspirin seem to be as effective in the treatment of arthritis as the far more costly steroids favoured by some vets. Brewer's yeast tablets have a high success rate for the treatment of rheumatism, with none of the side-effects associated with other treatments. Electro-magnets, enclosed in a special collar, are a newer treatment, and are winning many converts.

Constipation

Constipation is usually caused by an incorrect diet, and is distressing to the dog. Give milk of magnesia, but not too much as it can cause diarrhoea. If this does not solve the problem, consult your vet, who may prescribe a rectal suppository.

Diarrhoea

Shelties have a largely undeserved reputation for stomach upsets, perhaps because of the all-too-visible evidence of any problems on their profuse petticoats and tails. Diet is probably the most common cause of digestive problems. A Sheltie, like any other dog, thrives best on a regular and familiar routine, and changes of food may upset his digestive system. If you must, for any reason, change his diet, introduce a little of the new food by mixing it together with his regular food, and then gradually increase the quantity of the new food until the change is complete. Other causes of diarrhoea are intolerance of milk and other dairy products, over-excitement, and fear, especially of fireworks and other loud noises.

If diarrhoea persists for more than twenty-four hours, do not feed any solid food for the next twenty-four hours, but give unlimited access to fresh water. Do not let those pleading eyes divert you, as this temporary starvation is in the best interests of your dog. Introduce easily digested food, such as rice, fish, or chicken in small amounts for a few days until the faeces are consistently firm again, and then gradually return to a normal diet. Natural yoghurt is excellent for restoring the lining of the stomach and reintroducing the bacteria necessary to break down food. *Arsenicum album* is a homoeopathic remedy useful for mild diarrhoea. Diarrhoea that persists for more than twenty-four hours after food has been discontinued may have a more serious cause, and you should seek your vet's advice.

Eczema

This distressing skin condition is both irritating and painful. The skin is angry, red and weeping, with all the surrounding fur chewed away. Eczema appears most often at the bottom of the back, around the root of the tail, and along the flanks. These are all places that the dog can easily reach and nibble, and it is rarely seen in other places. The most common cause, and the simplest to correct, is diet. A food allergy, in particular an allergy to biscuit food, is often the culprit, and a change to a different and perhaps cheaper brand may be all that is needed to cure the problem.

Ineffective grooming is another prime cause of skin irritation. It is important to groom right down to the skin, regularly, to allow the air to reach the skin, and to remove any matted coat. Flea allergy also causes sore patches (*see* Parasites, below). Rescue Remedy (*see under* Shock, page 180) or Bob Grass ointment will promote healing.

Grass Seeds

Grass seeds are a serious menace in late summer. They cause intense irritation in the ears, but can also affect the feet. If a dog shows signs of irritation after exercise, check for grass seeds and remove them if you can. Otherwise consult your vet. Once in the body, the seeds travel and cause further problems. Keep grass in kennel runs and gardens cut short to prevent seeding, and be cautious when exercising dogs when grass is in seed.

Kennel Cough

This airborne virus is extremely infectious and, as its name suggests, is most often encountered where large numbers of dogs are kept in proximity. Boarding kennels and dog shows are thought to be particularly happy breeding grounds for the virus, but dogs that never leave their homes also become victims.

Sufferers have a dry, persistent, throaty cough that usually ends with a violent, explosive cough or dry retch. The owner often suspects, wrongly, that the dog has hairs or some other foreign body stuck in his throat. The strain of coughing can result in death for older dogs and puppies, so veterinary advice should be sought at an early stage. A homoeopathic remedy, *Bryonia*, may give relief, and vaccination is believed to afford some protection.

Metritus

Metritus is an infection of the uterus. The principal sources of infection are thought to be retained placentas or retained puppies. It can also occur if the uterine wall is lacerated during mating. Consult your vet if a bitch is unwell after whelping or mating.

Parasites

Ear Mites

Check a dog's ears as part of the grooming routine. Tiny black specks inside the ear flap are a sign of ear mites. Infested dogs also shake their heads and rub their ears on the ground. The vet will prescribe drops for treatment, and you should treat all the dogs and any cats that you have.

Fleas

If a dog persistently scratches himself, suspect fleas. They are notoriously difficult to detect in a densely coated dog, though the evidence is sometimes easier to see on the dog's underside. An obvious sign of infestation is the presence of small, gritty, dark brown particles in the coat. These are flea droppings, but may easily be mistaken for earth from the garden. A simple test is to add water to a sample held in cotton wool, which turns the droppings a distinctly red colour. Some dogs are extremely sensitive to flea bites. Symptoms of hypersensitivity, or 'flea allergy', are loss of hair and inflamed, red skin caused by excessive scratching. In such cases, Rescue Remedy (*see under* Shock, page 180) is effective in promoting healing, but you must of course ensure that the fleas are completely eradicated.

Pet shops sell shampoos, powders and sprays for treating dogs with fleas, and vets provide stronger, longer-lasting treatments on prescription. All dogs in the home or kennel should be treated at the same time. A dog's bedding and the house or kennel should also be treated with a proprietary spray especially formulated for use in the environment because fleas breed away from the dog in carpets, furnishings, and cracks in floorboards.

Ticks

Whether or not these are a problem depends on where you live. Town dogs may never pick them up, but dogs who exercise on grazing land may need checking for ticks every day.

Ticks are tiny when they first attach themselves to a dog, but when they bury their heads in a dog's skin in order to feed they swell up to look like a fat, grey or brown pea. They need to be removed carefully because an abscess can form if the head is left in. Dab the tick with ether or surgical spirit, then remove it with tweezers by twisting it away from the skin in an anti-clockwise direction. Then bathe the area with an antiseptic.

Worms

The commonest internal parasites are *Toxocara canis* roundworms. Infective *T. canis* larvae can be passed from bitch to puppy via the placenta during pregnancy, and afterwards via the bitch's milk. (This is why it is essential to worm puppies after whelping.) Eggs are also passed in the dog's faeces, where they become infective after two to three weeks. Other dogs (and humans) may ingest the eggs after contact with contaminated ground or an infected puppy.

184

Various types of tapeworm also affect dogs, the most common being *Dipylidium caninum*. This worm's intermediate host is the flea (it cannot be contracted directly), and so flea control plays an important part in preventing the occurrence of tapeworm.

Do not wait for signs of infestation: dogs should be wormed regularly with one of the wormers sold by vets and petshops. The frequency of worming depends on the individual product. Always consult your vet before worming a bitch in whelp.

Thyroid Imbalance

Thyroid imbalance may be more common in all breeds of dogs than many people suspect. It is thought by some medical experts to be strongly linked to areas of high radioactivity, and is far more common in bitches than in dogs. A simple blood test shows if the thyroid is over- or under-active. A bitch with an under-active thyroid may not ovulate, and becomes extremely lethargic and overweight. Her coat is probably less luxuriant and has a greasy feel, perhaps only down the spinal area, or all over. An over-active thyroid causes an animal to be hyperactive and lose weight despite having a robust appetite. The imbalance is corrected by the daily administration of tablets from the vet.

Useful Addresses

Kennel Clubs

Australian National Kennel Council
PO Box 285
Red Hill South
Victoria 3937
Australia
Tel. 00-61/015 304 338

The Kennel Club
1–5 Clarges Street
Piccadilly
London
W1Y 8AB
UK
Tel. 0171 493 6651

FCI, Fédération Cynologique Internationale
12 Rue Leopold II
B-6530 Thuin
Belgium

Shetland Sheepdog Clubs of Great Britain

Eastern Counties Shetland Sheepdog Club
Mrs C. Aaron
Home Farm
Bull Road
Pakenham
Suffolk IP31 2LW

English Shetland Sheepdog Club
Mrs E. Gibbens
254 Woolwich Road
Abbey Wood
London SE2 0DW

**Mid Western Shetland
  Sheepdog Club**
Mr C. Mayhew
36 The Chestnuts
Hinstock
Shropshire TF9 2SX

**Northern Counties Shetland
  Sheepdog Club**
Miss M. Gatheral
Sockburn Hall
Neasham
Darlington
Co. Durham DL12 1PH

**Scottish Shetland Sheepdog
  Club**
Mrs M. Anderson
Vaila
Ayr Road
Irvine
Ayrshire KA11 5AB

**Shetland Sheepdog Club of
  North Wales**
Mr D. Hulme
45 Dolwen Road
Old Colwyn
Clwyd LL29 8UP

**Shetland Sheepdog Club of
  Northern Ireland**
Mr A. Morrison
19 Ballyhill Road
Belfast BT14 8SI

**Shetland Sheepdog Club of
  Wales**
Mrs V. Dyer
Waterend Cottage
Hayes End
Longney
Gloucestershire GL2 6SW

**Yorkshire Shetland Sheepdog
  Club**
Mrs B. Butler
8 Drake Close
Burncross
Sheffield S30 4TB

Further Reading

Baker, Maurice, *Shetland Sheepdogs Today* (Ringpress Ltd, 1988).

Combe, Iris, *Herding Dogs. Their Origins and Development in Britain* (Faber and Faber, 1987).

Davis, Mary, *Shetland Sheepdogs* (Arthur Barker Ltd, 1973).

Gwynne-Jones, Olwen, *The Shetland Sheepdog Handbook* (Nicholson & Watson, London, 1958).

Moody, Jan, *Shetland Sheepdogs – The Sheltie* (Bredicot Publications, 1990).

Osborne, Margaret, *The Popular Shetland Sheepdog* (Popular Dogs, 1959).

Rogers, Felicity M., *All About The Shetland Sheepdog* (Pelham Books, 1980).

Smythe R.H., M.R.C.V.S., *The Dog: Structure and Movement* (W. Foulsham & Co. Ltd, 1970).

Thynne, Beryl, *The Shetland Sheepdog* (Illustrated Kennel News, 1916. Republished by Dogs in Print, 1990).

Watson, Mark, *The Iceland Dog 874–1956* (published privately).

Index